SCAPEGOATS

How Islamophobia Helps Our Enemies and Threatens Our Freedoms

ARSALAN IFTIKHAR

FOREWORD BY REZA ALSAN

Hot Books

Hot Books may be purchased in bulk at special discounts for sales promotion, corporate gifts, fund-raising, or educational purposes. Special editions can also be created to specifications. For details, contact the Special Sales Department, Skyhorse Publishing, 307 West 36th Street, 11th Floor, New York, NY 10018 or info@skyhorsepublishing.com.

Hot Books® and Skyhorse Publishing® are registered trademarks of Skyhorse Publishing, Inc.®, a Delaware corporation.

Visit our website at www.skyhorsepublishing.com.

10 9 8 7 6 5 4 3 2 1

Library of Congress Cataloging-in-Publication Data is available on file.

Cover design by Brian Peterson

Print ISBN: 978-1-5107-0575-3
Ebook ISBN: 978-1-5107-0579-1

Printed in the United States of America

Table of Contents

Foreword

By Reza Aslan

A June 2015 front-page article in *The New York Times* noted that since 9/11 more than twice as many Americans have been killed in acts of domestic terrorism by "white supremacists" than by Islamic extremists. That figure, it should be noted, does not include school shootings, which have tragically become nearly regular episodes in the United States.

It does not include the actions of mass murderers like Dylann Roof, the 21-year-old white supremacist who killed nine African-American worshippers at a historic Charleston, South Carolina, church; or Wade Michael Page, who walked into a Sikh temple in Oak Creek, Wisconsin, and murdered six worshippers, presumably because he thought they were Muslims. Nor does it include Robert Dear, the Christian zealot who attacked a Planned Parenthood clinic in Colorado, shooting to death a police officer and two others. And it most certainly does not include Bob Doggart, the Christian pastor from Tennessee who was arrested planning a mass slaughter of Muslims in New York.

According to the FBI, more Americans will die because of "faulty furniture" than at the hands of Islamic terrorists. Your flat-screen television is a greater threat to your life than either ISIS or al-Qaeda. Of course, one would never know any of this based on the words of our politicians and media personalities today. In their view, every Muslim is a closet jihadist just waiting for the opportunity to bring down Western civilization as we know it today.

It is hard to blame the media alone for this phenomenon. After all, the media is in the consumer entertainment business. They actively portray tiny fringe elements within Islam as representative of all Muslims because fear sells their products. And politicians have always benefited from stoking fear and xenophobia, and will continue to do so as long as there is such a thing as politics. Nevertheless, the result of all this fear mongering for votes and profit is that Islamophobia has now become a perfectly accepted form of religious bigotry in Western societies today.

There are, of course, those who insist that there is no such thing as Islamophobia, that it is merely a means of warding off legitimate criticism of Islam. *The National Review*, the conservative journal, has called Islamophobia "a myth." The celebrated anti-theist ideologue Sam Harris likes to say that Islamophobia is "a word created by fascists, and used by cowards, to manipulate morons." Such arguments are based on a confused combination of tortured semantics and a stubborn refusal to recognize that negative sentiments toward Muslims represent a form of bigotry.

Yet, since bigotry is not a rational response but an emotional one—a result of fear, not ignorance—thinking of anti-Muslim bigotry as a "phobia" should then make perfect sense, especially when one is confronted with daily attacks against Muslim individuals, mosques, schools, and cemeteries around the world.

The fact of the matter is that less than half of Americans say they personally know a Muslim and so most people rely on the media to shape their opinions about Islam and Muslims.

That is the problem.

Because as every social scientist knows, it is not data that change people's minds. What will change people's minds about disenfranchised groups are human relationships. The more humanized a disenfranchised group becomes to a society, the more difficult it is to demonize that group.

In the meantime, the impact of unfettered Islamophobia is leading many Western societies down a dark path. In

Europe, we are witnessing the passage of laws curtailing the rights and freedoms of Muslim communities. We are also witnessing the electoral success of blatantly anti-Muslim political parties, which further leads to a sense of marginalization among Europe's diverse Muslim communities. That, in turn, is leading to severe alienation among some of Europe's increasingly disenfranchised Muslim youth in the future. This process of turning Muslims into the "dangerous outsider" only became more intense after the Paris terror attacks in November 2015.

The same kind of Islamophobia that has made much of Europe inhospitable to its Muslim citizens is now threatening to further alienate American Muslims as well. An entire generation of young Muslim kids born here in the United States after 9/11 is now living with the unique experience of facing discrimination under the guise of liberalism and liberation. And the bigotry has only gotten worse over the years, particularly with the vicious rhetoric of the 2016 Republican presidential campaign.

Islamophobia is troubling, but its trajectory in this country is not unique. If we look at statements being made about Muslims in this country—that they are somehow un-American, that they do not represent American values, that they are "foreign," that they are exotic, that they are the quintessential "other"—we find the same exact statements being made about Catholic and Jewish people in our recent history as well.

Muslims just happen to be the newest outsider group in this country. What's more, anti-Muslim sentiment in the United States is very much connected to anti immigrant sentiment. Even though Muslims came to America as slaves long before the establishment of this country, nearly two-thirds of American Muslims are first-generation immigrants. Yet at the same time, nearly 70 percent of those Muslim immigrants are American citizens. That's the highest citizenship rate of any immigrant community in America.

If there is a silver lining about the growth of Islamophobia in this country it is that it is reinvigorating our Western societal discourses on the intersection of media, journalism, politics, and faith. That is what makes *Scapegoats: How Islamophobia Helps Our Enemies and Threatens Our Freedoms*—which exhaustively chronicles the narrative history of Islamophobia after September 11—such an important book. It should be read by anyone who is interested in correcting the mistakes of our collective past to ensure a brighter shared tomorrow for our future generations.

Dr. Reza Aslan is an internationally acclaimed scholar of religions and author of the #1 *New York Times* Bestseller *Zealot: The Life and Times of Jesus of Nazareth* and the international best-seller *No god but God: The Origins, Evolution, and Future of Islam.*

Introduction

"Terrorism . . . The word that means nothing, yet justifies everything."

—Glenn Greenwald

As I was preparing to submit my first draft of this book to my publisher, I began to hear breaking news about the November 2015 terrorist attacks in Paris, which ultimately claimed 130 innocent lives. For the next week, I spent all my time running between TV and radio studios here in Washington, D.C., doing interviews with Anderson Cooper on CNN, Chuck Todd and fellow panelist Tom Brokaw on NBC's *Meet the Press,* on ABC News *Nightline* and National Public

Radio, as well as on overseas networks like Al-Jazeera English (twice in three days) and CCTV, the largest English-language television news network in China. That was just in one week alone.

Then, just as I was finishing my revisions on the book, news broke about the December 2015 mass shooting in San Bernardino, California, where a husband and wife Muslim couple named Syed Rizwan Farook and Tashfeen Malik murdered fourteen people in cold blood during a holiday party for the San Bernardino County health department where the husband worked. As the American public reeled from the latest explosion of mass violence—this one in an otherwise unremarkable suburban California community—the media was once again dominated by discussion of the purported "Muslim" nature of the mass murder. Lost in the all the frantic chatter about San Bernardino was the revelation that the male shooter, Rizwan Farook, had stopped going to mosque over two years prior to the bloodbath, and that one of his victims was a female Muslim colleague who actually attended the same mosque as the shooter once did. It also turned out that the killer's own brother, Raheel Farook, is a decorated US Navy veteran, who has been awarded the National Defense Service Medal, Global War on Terrorism Expeditionary Medal and Global War on Terrorism Service Medal.

As with the Paris attacks less than three weeks before, I was again swept up in the media frenzy, asked to appear yet again on CNN, BBC World News, Al-Jazeera English, NPR, and ABC. Again, that was in just one week after San Bernardino.

Welcome to the life of a Muslim public intellectual in post-9/11, post-Paris, post-San Bernardino, and post-whatever-comes-next-in-the-world. When irresponsible political leaders and media talking heads rush to demonize Islam and lump all Muslims—all 1.7 billion of us—with murderous terrorists, it falls to a few "go-to" professional Muslim public intellectuals like me to try to talk America down from that precipice ledge of hysteria. *We're not all terrorists, we're a peace-loving religion, we condemn the destruction of innocent lives.* And so on, and so on, and so on . . .

My life really began at 8:46 a.m. Eastern Standard Time on September 11, 2001. Because that was the exact moment in time when my country was attacked by people who simultaneously also hijacked my religion. Ever since that fateful day, it would be accurate to say that my entire existence has revolved around presenting a genuine Muslim voice in the mainstream media at a time in modern history when so much of the global narrative about Islam and Muslims revolves around olive-skinned, gun-toting bearded men who look a lot like Osama bin Laden. The remainder of my life will probably turn into one big absurd game of TV musical chairs and YouTube video clips, as I sit in one media "hot seat" after the next, trying my best to inform the public that 1.7 billion mainstream Muslims will not be represented by bobble-headed terrorists with idiot names like Boko Haram and ISIS.

During my numerous media interviews following Paris and San Bernardino, I tried to highlight that in the year 2015 alone, there were over 350 mass shootings in the United States and that 99 percent of these mass shootings were not committed by Muslims. There is nothing "Islamic" about acts of vicious mayhem and wanton murder like Paris and San Bernardino, I say again and again into cameras and microphones around the world. Those who have killed innocent people in places like Paris, London, and Madrid—as well as in more remote places like Mali, Nigeria, and Kenya that the Western media don't seem quite as concerned about—are nothing more than godless maniacs, who often wantonly kill more Muslims than they do members of other religions. No matter where these terrorists do their sinister work, I loudly declaim whenever I'm interviewed, these brainwashed idiots have clearly lost their bloody minds and are committing irreligious acts of mass murder that have nothing to do with the true mainstream teachings of a 1,400-year-old religion called Islam, which over a billion and a half people throughout the world practice peacefully every day.

I have repeated this message again and again, year after year—as do other "go-to" Muslim public intel lectuals favored by the media, like my good friend, the best-selling author Reza Aslan. But I have come to despair that anyone is actually listening to us. Whenever some violent lunatic snaps and claims some kind of warped justification for his murderous acts as a so-called Muslim warrior, it's not his damaged childhood or the flood of assault weapons in America or the climate of unrelenting violence in our country that gets blamed— it's Islam, an ancient, Abrahamic religion with centuries of civilizational contributions (like the invention of algebra and medical anesthesia) and peaceful coexistence with diverse peoples around the world.

This collective response to atrocities like Paris and San Bernardino has become so reflexive within our Western culture that we don't even question its fundamental absurdity. To see the obviously unfair and unreasonable terrorism double standard at work here, all one has to do is compare the coverage of these terror incidents with the explosions of violence perpetrated by madmen like Robert Dear, the anti-abortion Christian terrorist who shot up the Planned Parenthood clinic in Colorado around the same time as Paris and San Bernardino because of his own warped religious ideology. Dear was known for strongly espousing fundamentalist Christian beliefs. His ex-wife once testified in court that he "claims to be a Christian and is extremely evangelistic. . . . He says that as long as he believes he will be saved, he can do whatever he pleases." In his own deranged mind, Dear's actions were undoubtedly justified by his warped version of Christianist ideology. And, yet, following Robert Dear's bloody rampage, TV news producers did not feel compelled to book Christian preachers or prominent Protestants and Catholics on their shows and ask them to condemn the Planned Parenthood attack as an act of Christian terrorism.

It should also be noted that Dear's violent actions were directed against Planned Parenthood, an organization that had been recently demonized in the overheated Republican presidential campaign as a group that peddled "baby parts." Dear even made reference to this false and inflammatory political charge as he went about his homicidal mission that day. But again, Dear's murder spree was not covered by the media as an act of terrorism, even though it clearly had a politicized target.

Or consider Dylann Roof—the twenty-one-year-old white supremacist who a few months earlier, on the evening of June 17, 2015, walked into the Emanuel African Methodist Episcopal Church in Charleston, South Carolina, with a .45-caliber Glock handgun. After sitting with the black church's congregants for over an hour during their Bible study class, Roof then proceeded to systematically execute nine African-American worshippers in cold blood, including South Carolina state senator Clementa Pinckney, whom he specifically had asked for by name before committing this savage act of domestic terrorism.

By his own admission, Dylann Roof's act was racially motivated since he had stated that he wanted to start a "race war" before his terrorist rampage. Before opening fire, Roof had told his innocent victims, "I have to do it. . . . You rape our women and you're taking over our country." In a photograph he posted on social media, the gunman wore the flags of formerly white-ruled apartheid South Africa and Rhodesia. His friends described him as a person who regularly made racist remarks and his roommate admitted that Roof was planning something like his massacre of black churchgoers for six months before he walked into the Charleston prayer meeting.

But, like anti-abortion religious zealot Robert Dear, Dylann Roof was never called a terrorist in the media either. In fact, after his act of bloody mayhem, Roof was treated with remarkable care by the arresting police officers, who took him to a Burger King before booking him when he complained he was hungry. It is not hard to imagine how the police in South Carolina would have responded if a black gunman or a shooter fitting the "Muslim terrorist" profile had walked into a prayer meeting at a white church and shot up the congregation.

Simply put, the term "terrorism" has come to be applied within our Western societies only when Muslims commit acts of mass murder. And the so-called war on terror has come to justify rising levels of violence and persecution aimed at Muslims at home and abroad. But the truth is, whether it is a mass shooting at a holiday party in San Bernardino or a Planned Parenthood clinic in Colorado or a black church in South Carolina, these are all acts of *American* terrorism. The perpetrators in all three cases were Americans and their innocent victims represented the rainbow diversity of America, including men and women of all races, religions, and ethnicities. The killers were driven to act not just by their own damaged psyches, but out of some warped response to the tensions within American society. And they all were able to commit mass murder because of America's fatal addiction to guns.

Terrorism is not the exclusive property of those who claim to embrace Islam. Horrifying acts of violence against innocent civilians have been inflicted by a wide range of individuals (and government officials) who claim all sorts of lofty justification for their vile acts of murder. And yet it is Islam that has become exclusively conflated with terrorism in the public mind. This dangerously skewed image of Muslims began to take hold in America after 9/11 and has only become worse, particularly during the savage primary season of 2016 Republican presidential politics, when Muslim-bashing became standard fare on the campaign trail.

A few years ago, the Gallup Center for Muslim Studies released a comprehensive public opinion study entitled "Muslim Americans: Faith, Freedom, and the Future," which gave a fascinating look at how Muslim Americans were viewed by other religious groups in the United States nearly a decade after 9/11. Since this book posits that Islam is certainly the most misunderstood (and vilified) religion in America today, it should come as little surprise that this Gallup study found that over 37 percent of American Protestants, 35 percent of Catholics, and 32 percent of Mormons across the United States believed that Muslim Americans are "not loyal citizens to America." In contrast, many people might be surprised to learn that over 80 percent of Jewish Americans showed solidarity with followers of Islam, telling the Gallup pollsters that American Muslims are actually loyal citizens and not a threat to the United States.

Furthermore, according to this Gallup study, nearly 60 percent of American Muslims stated that they experienced overt prejudice from other Americans. (Nearly 66 percent of Jewish Americans, who historically have felt the same sting of prejudice, agreed that most Americans harbor some bias against Muslims in general.) In addition, nearly half of the American Muslims polled in the report declared that they had faced some form of "racial profiling or religious discrimination" within the last year alone.

Since this poll was conducted by Gallup in 2011, the situation has only grown grimmer since that time. Following the San Bernardino mayhem, a mosque in a nearby community was firebombed and other Islamic religious centers across the country became targets of a new wave of anti-Muslim violence. According to the Center for the Study of Hate and Extremism at California State University, San Bernardino, the average number of monthly hate crimes against Muslims— including arsons and vandalism aimed at Islamic institutions, death threats, and assaults on hijab-wearing women and others—has tripled since the Paris and San Bernardino terror attacks. Hours after the shootings in San Bernardino, reported *The New York Times*, "kill Muslims" became the top Google search in California with the word "Muslims" in it, as well as one of the most popular search requests nationwide.

Because of increased Islamophobia in the West today, many young Muslims in the United States and Europe now feel like "strangers in a strange land" in the countries of their birth—simply because of their brown skin, foreign-sounding names, and Islamic religious affiliation.

Here in America, at least thirty out of fifty states have proposed some kind of discriminatory "anti-Sharia" legislation, as a result of fear campaigns based on the absurd notion that the American legal system is in danger of being replaced by traditional Islamic laws. We have seen hate campaigns going viral, like that of the publicity-hungry, Quran-burning pastor in Florida who looks like a wild-eyed character straight out of *Sons of Anarchy*. We have witnessed "anti-mosque" movements popping up everywhere from Sheboygan, Wisconsin, to Temecula, California, trying to stop houses of worship being built by local citizens. And, most tragically, we have seen death threats and hate crimes directed against Muslim Americans simply because of their faith all across the country.

The inflamed anti-Muslim rhetoric that now fills the airwaves only raises the level of danger. This hate language spews from across the political spectrum—whether it comes from 2016 Republican presidential candidate Donald Trump and his outrageous calls for registering American Muslims and banning all members of the Islamic faith from entering the United States, or from self-proclaimed "liberal" comedian Bill Maher, who routinely disparages Islam as a backward and dangerous religion and invites anti-Muslim propagandists on his HBO show, *Real Time*, to do the same.

There is one very simple message that I would like to convey to every Islamophobe on behalf of world peace.

Your inflammatory statements only help to increase recruitment for groups like ISIS and al-Qaeda, because these militants will play your vicious and derogatory video clips to young and disenfranchised potential recruits to prove that the Western world hates Muslims. What do you think you are accomplishing by venting your ill-informed and poisonous opinions? You are certainly not making it any easier for the vast majority of mainstream and level-headed Muslim thought leaders who are trying their hardest to keep an already very heated situation from boiling over. When you make stupid, bigoted, and xenophobic statements like "All Muslims are evil" or "Islam is a wicked religion," you have joined our enemies on the dark side, where you all feel free to wallow in the basest of human emotions.

And by the way, when crazed jihadists do decide to strike out against perceived Western injustices by killing innocent people, it is predominantly Muslim civilians themselves who suffer the most—not the people tuning in to right-wing talk radio in America. Most studies show that over 90 percent of jihadi terrorist victims worldwide are Muslims themselves. This is why it must be shouted from the rooftops and minarets of the world that there is no other group in the world who hates violent Islamists more than mainstream Muslims ourselves. Not only are these self-proclaimed "holy warriors" simply mass-murdering criminals with no sense of humanity, but they have tried to steal a beautiful faith that comforts millions around the world in order to further their perverted agenda. On behalf of Muslims worldwide, I tell my fellow Americans: you simply cannot hate these murderers more than we ourselves hate them.

As a prominent Muslim journalist, this is why I am so determined to shift the narrative away from these killers with their repulsive spectacles of violence and focus on the achievements of our diverse Muslim communities around the world. We need to highlight the many Muslims who do amazing things—like Malala Yousufzai, Shirin Ebadi, Mohamed El-Baradei, Tawakkul Karman, and Mohammed Younus, who have won five out of the last twelve Nobel Peace Prizes.

We need to highlight the work of the next generation of forward-thinking Islamic religious scholars like Egypt's Moez Masoud, Khalid Latif, and Suhaib Webb from the United States, and Yemen's Habib Ali Jifri—thinkers who can effectively speak to the new generation of Muslims. We also need our Western Muslim celebrities, athletes, and entrepreneurs—such as Kareem Abdul-Jabbar, Muhammad Ali, Dave Chappelle, Aziz Ansari, and Salman Khan—to help show our alienated Western Muslim youth that there are many different ways that you can contribute to society without having to join dystopic death cults posing as true believers.

As one of these diverse, mainstream voices from the new generation of Muslim thought leaders, I will continue to do my part. I will continue to take my proverbial hot seat in frigid television studios, where I will keep countering the messages of hate and intolerance coming from all directions, including the illiberal left and the neoconservative right. And I will continue to wonder if God will ever forgive us for what we have done to each other.

Chapter One

When Life Gives You a (Don) Lemon . . .

L ike virtually all Americans, my life changed forever on September 11, 2001—but in a most unique way. Born and raised in the United States, I proudly grew up in my hometown of Chicago and proceeded to receive my "Top 20" education at Washington University in St. Louis, where I received both my undergraduate and law degrees, focusing on international human rights law. But suddenly after 9/11, I immediately became "the Muslim Guy"—one of the go-to pundits that the American media turned to in its fumbling effort to understand the more than one-and-a-half billion people around the world who are believers in Islam. But my life as a Muslim public figure did not truly get turned upside down until the evening of January 7, 2015, when I was invited to go on-air with CNN anchor Don Lemon to discuss that day's terror attack at the offices of the French satirical magazine *Charlie Hebdo*.

As millions of CNN viewers around the world witnessed, it was during this now-famous interview when Don Lemon bizarrely asked me the question, "Do you support ISIS?"—simply because I am a Muslim. This surreal question—and my stunned, outraged reaction—instantly went viral, destined to become immortalized as one of those prime examples of media cluelessness that forever define a historical moment.

First of all, Don Lemon's question caught me off-guard because, *hello*, I'm a HUMAN RIGHTS LAWYER. I've spent my entire career fighting for values that are antithetical to those of the ruthless terror group. Second, as millions of CNN viewers who watched my interview that evening can vouch, I had devoted nearly the entire interview (almost five minutes out of a total six) categorically condemning that morning's Paris terrorist attack, using the most vehement terms that can be found in the English language today.

From the very beginning of my now-infamous interview, I started by telling Lemon that I was "shocked and horrified" at the Paris attack and that it was "against any normative teaching of Islam." Continuing in this outraged vein, I told Lemon that the Paris terrorists were "irreligious criminals committing acts of mass murder" and that the bloodshed they perpetrated was a "crime against humanity."

How much more condemnation do you need from a Muslim public intellectual?

But apparently these resounding rebukes of the *Charlie Hebdo* terrorists were not enough for the CNN anchor. As the interview entered its final minute, Lemon asked me about some obscure Russian public opinion poll that claimed that 16 percent of French Muslims felt sympathy for ISIS, the notorious terrorist network, and then proceeded to ask me the question heard around the world: *Do you support ISIS?*

Now to be completely honest with you, I thought that I had misheard Don Lemon's question. Surely, it was not possible that any national TV anchor would be dumb enough to ask a human rights lawyer this question. But then I remembered that I was dealing with Don Lemon, a TV host known for his off-the-wall questions. And I was filled with a rush of indignation. "Wait," I said. "Did you just ask if I support ISIS?"

This was the absolute extent of the response that I was going to give such a blatantly ridiculous question. Such a patently absurd question did not deserve to be dignified with any more of a reply.

Thankfully, this is where the Internet took over.

In less than twenty-four hours, over five thousand articles blossomed online, blasting Lemon for his asinine question, in American publications as disparate as *USA Today, BuzzFeed, Deadspin,* and *The Hollywood Reporter,* and hundreds more around the world. *USA Today* wryly observed that "the saying 'There is no such thing as a dumb question' may not apply" to Lemon's interview with me the night before. Meanwhile, Professor Shaheen Pasha of the University of Massachusetts-Amherst noted in a tweet that the "CNN version of a Fox News anchor [Don Lemon] just asked human rights attorney Arsalan Iftikhar if he supports ISIS. . . . Head just exploded." And Dave Zirin of *The Nation* magazine commented that "Asking Arsalan—author of the book *Islamic Pacifism*—if he supports ISIS is like confusing Angela Davis with Condi Rice. . . . If Don Lemon had interviewed Nelson Mandela, he would've demanded to know where he stood on Iggy Azalea."

The vast majority of these five-thousand-plus articles pointed out that his ISIS question to me was just the latest in a series of major Don Lemon on-air gaffes, including his suggestion that Malaysia Airlines Flight 370 might have flown into a "black hole" ("I know it's preposterous . . . but is it preposterous?" he inanely remarked after the plane disappeared), or the time he asked an alleged Bill Cosby rape victim why she did not chomp down on the comedian's penis while he was forcing himself on her. "There are ways not to perform oral sex if you didn't want to do it," Lemon weirdly advised the woman. "You know, meaning the use of teeth, right?"

So I was not the only CNN guest to be drawn into Don Lemon's bizarre alternate reality. Still, it is a deeply unnerving experience to be suddenly associated with international terrorism on national television after a career spent upholding international law and human rights—simply because of my religion.

There were expressions of support for me from across the political spectrum—including from Glenn Greenwald on the left and from former Republican National Committee (RNC) chairman (and my dear friend) Michael Steele, who immediately tweeted: "Human rights lawyer Arsalan Iftikhar interview [with Don Lemon] is a stunning insult to his work and advocacy." It was enormously comforting to hear these words of support from people on both sides of the political aisle.

But the fact is that Muslims, Arabs, and South Asians are under severe attack from all directions in the West these days. In Western countries where freedom of religion is built into their very constitutional bedrock, one of the great religions of the world is being increasingly criminalized. Republican candidates compete with each other to propose the most authoritarian measures and to use the most incendiary language to deal with the so-called Muslim problem. Muslim men and women are physically attacked and even murdered. Mosques in American cities are vandalized and desecrated. Hate speech that would never be tolerated against other groups—including African Americans, Jews, gays, or women—is given free license in the media, and not just on the predictably strident Fox News shows but on "liberal" HBO as well.

Earlier in my interview with Don Lemon, I spoke out against this demonization of Islam. "It's important not to conflate the actions of a very few (criminals) with a population of 1.7 billion people, which represents 20 percent of the world's population," I remarked. "You know, if people want to blame Islam for things . . . they can blame us for inventing algebra or modern medical anesthesia or having five out of the last twelve Nobel Peace Prize winners.

"When Christians commit acts of terror, we don't asks priests and pastors to go on national television to condemn these acts," I also said that night on CNN. "But sadly, Muslim public intellectuals, thinkers, leaders, and Islamic scholars have that double standard that we have to deal with. . . . I think it's important to keep in mind that bringing religion into it at all is actually serving the purposes of the terrorists."

Professor Juan Cole of the University of Michigan has taken up this same theme—the double standard applied to acts of terrorism committed by professed Muslims and those carried out by Christians. "[Oklahoma City bombers] Timothy McVeigh and Terry Nichols would never be called 'Christian terrorists' even though they were in close contact with the Christian Identity Movement," observed Professor Cole. "No one would speak of Christo-fascism or Judeo-fascism as the Republican[s] . . . speak of 'Islamo-fascism.' [In fact, it was] persons of Christian heritage [who] invented fascism, not Muslims."

Dangerous demagogues throughout history have sought to reinforce their rule by frightening the public and creating scapegoats on whom to focus their fears and resentments. The Catholic and Jewish scapegoats of an earlier era have become the Muslim scapegoats of today. There is no more logic for this demonization of Muslims today than there was for innocent Jewish people in Nazi Germany or African Americans in the Jim Crow South, or for that matter in our cities of today, where blacks have long been a target of police brutality and systemic violence.

This book is an effort to shed some light and reason at a time when our Western public life seems to have very little of either. We need to call out those xenophobes who are exploiting fear and hatred and push back against the language of intolerance that is spreading so widely in the political arena and in our media echo chambers. History has taught us that when a group of people are dehumanized by public rhetoric and turned into the proverbial "other," we usually see that tragic societal consequences often follow. As Americans with a deep pluralistic tradition of respect for political, ethnic, and religious diversity, we must now invoke the better angels of our nature . . . before it's too late.

Chapter Two

The Media Crusade Against Islam

Mohammed Salman Hamdani was a twenty-three-year-old New York City police cadet who was one of the 2,976 people who tragically died on September 11, 2001, trying to save fellow New Yorkers in the World Trade Center on that fateful day. But strangely enough, fifteen fifteen years later, Hamdani's name is still nowhere to be found in the long list of fallen first responders at the National September 11 Memorial in lower Manhattan.

Hamdani's mother has always been convinced that her son's Islamic religion is what set him apart from the other heroes who died on 9/11. "They do not want anyone with a Muslim name to be acknowledged at Ground Zero with such high honors," Talat Hamdani told *The*

9

New York Times. "They don't want someone with the name Mohammad to be up there."

She is undoubtedly right.

Even though Mohammad Hamdani was an all-American kid who played high school football, eventually became a certified emergency medical technician (EMT), and loved the *Star Wars* movie trilogy, the moment that he went missing on 9/11 trying to save lives, the anti-Muslim conspiracy theories began to swirl. "Some people continued to see him as something he was not," noted *The New York Times.* "After [23-year-old] Mr. Hamdani disappeared on Sept. 11, ugly rumors circulated: he was a Muslim and worked in a lab; he might have been connected to a terrorist group." According to other media reports, flyers were circulated around the city stating that Hamdani was wanted for questioning by the Joint Terrorism Task Force. To add insult to injury, the Rupert Murdoch–owned *New York Post* ran a prominent story on Hamdani's disappearance next to his photo with the sinister headline: "Missing—Or Hiding?"

Several months later, the truth about Mohammed Salman Hamdani finally came out. Law enforcement officials said that the young man's charred remains had been found near the north tower of the World Trade Center complex, where he had bravely gone to rescue fellow Americans whom he had never met before. "And then, at last, everyone could see Mr. Hamdani for what he truly was," *The New York Times* concluded. "An American hero."

There were also Muslim heroes during the recent explosions of terrorist violence in Paris, including Ahmed Merabet, a French police officer who died trying to stop the gunmen responsible for the *Charlie Hebdo* magazine attack, and Lassana Bathily, a Muslim immigrant who helped save the lives of several customers during the deadly assault on a kosher Jewish supermarket that was part of the same spasm of terror. "I helped Jews [because] we're all brothers," the Muslim immigrant told the press afterward. But none of this heroism and human solidarity has slowed down the raging Islamophobia that only burns more fiercely each time a violent extremist tries to condone his actions by invoking one of the world's great religions.

As I stated in a 2010 *Time* magazine cover story, "Islamophobia has become the accepted form of racism in America. . . . You can always take a potshot at Muslims or Arabs and get away with it." In that *Time* article, I predicted we will continue to see many political leaders in the Western world successfully use anti-Muslim sentiment as a wedge issue to stir up the worst human passions and win votes. This ugly, demagogic rhetoric reached a new low during the 2016 Republican presidential campaign, as GOP contenders such as Donald Trump, Ben Carson, and Ted Cruz competed with each other to command the Muslim-bashing heights (or depths).

Trump won the bigotry prize with his calls for barring all Muslims from entering the United States and registering all Muslim Americans—a proposal that called to mind the yellow Star of David badges that Jewish people in Nazi-controlled Europe were forced to wear. But virtually the entire GOP pack flaunted its flaming prejudice.

Unfortunately, this frenzied intolerance is nothing new. Conservative evangelical preachers in the United States have long been exploiting anti-Muslims biases for short-term political gain. Senator John McCain once rightfully referred to these men of the cloth as "agents of intolerance" since many of these self-proclaimed "Christian" leaders have helped give our collective anti-Muslim societal animus a righteous justification.

One of the most offensive such preachers is the legendary Reverend Billy Graham's son, Franklin. The younger Graham infamously declared during a November 2001 broadcast of *NBC Nightly News with Tom Brokaw* that Islam is a "very wicked and evil religion . . . not of the same God." Graham continued his crusade against Islam in a 2005 interview with CNN host Anderson Cooper in which he bizarrely claimed that the only way that Muslims could attain salvation was through dying in a holy war. Graham followed this outburst four years later with another outrageous CNN interview during which

he tarbrushed all Muslims as fundamentalist fanatics—
an ironic accusation considering his own religious zealotry. "True Islam cannot be practiced in this country,"
Graham stated. "You can't beat your wife. You cannot
murder your children if you think they've committed
adultery or something like that, which they do practice
in these [Muslim] countries."

Graham has also publicly protested the construction
of the Park51 Community Center in lower Manhattan
(pejoratively referred to as the "Ground Zero Mosque")
by suggesting that Muslims "will claim now that the
World Trade Center property is Islamic land." During
an October 2010 ABC town hall event, Graham insisted
that American Muslims "want to build as many mosques
and cultural centers as they possibly can so they can convert as many Americans as they can to Islam." Finally,
it would not truly be modern-day Islamophobia without Franklin Graham jumping on board the right-wing
conspiratorial bandwagon and publicly stating that
President Barack Obama was "born a Muslim."

Graham has never apologized for hurling insults at
a 1,400-year-old religious faith followed by nearly one-
fifth of the world's population. But his own father was
forced to eventually distance himself from his son's blatant Islamophobia during an August 2006 interview with
Newsweek magazine. "I would not say Islam is wicked
and evil," said the elder Billy Graham. "I have a lot of

friends who are Islamic. There are many wonderful people among them. I have a great love for them. . . . I'm sure
there are many things that [my son Franklin] and I are
not in total agreement about." It was a rare expression of
interfaith tolerance from a leading evangelical leader.

Franklin Graham is far from the only fundamentalist leader who regularly calls down fire and brim-
stone on the Islamic faith. Reverend Pat Robertson, the
octogenarian evangelical polemicist who helped found
the Christian Coalition, has also spent many years
spewing anti-Muslim rhetoric through his Christian
Broadcasting Network (CBN) television channel and
its flagship television show, *The 700 Club*. During his
seemingly never-ending tenure at CBN, Robertson has
stated that Islam is a "satanic" religion that is motivated
by "demonic power" and is "not a religion of peace."

During a May 2005 appearance on ABC News' *This
Week with George Stephanopoulos*, the elderly bible-
thumper took his Islamophobia to new heights when he
opposed appointing Muslims and Hindus to top posi-
tions in the American government or judiciary.

Whenever Muslims are collectively thrown on the
bonfire, Pat Robertson is generally among the first
to pop up with a torch. In December 2015, as Donald
Trump fanned the flames of modern-day fascism with
his calls to target all Muslims as potential enemies,
Robertson soon joined in this un-Christian orgy of

hatred. It was okay to persecute Muslims, Robertson assured his television faithful, because Islam "isn't a religion as such . . . [It] is actually a political system that is bent on dominating you and killing you."

But even the shockingly intemperate rhetoric issuing forth from conservative Christian pulpits cannot match the vicious language of the right-wing punditocracy. Ann Coulter set the rabid tone shortly after 9/11 when she suggested that we "should invade their countries, kill their leaders and convert them to Christianity." Ever since then, Coulter has become one of the West's most-infamous anti-Muslim voices, with her hate speech being given a prominent platform not just on FOX News but on Bill Maher's "liberal" *Real Time* program on HBO as well. Coulter has called for "mass deportation" of Muslims from America. In response to critcisms of her support for racially profiling Muslims, she has declared that our American motto should be: "Raghead talks tough . . . Raghead faces consequences." (Imagine the response if a media personality was allowed to spew the same hateful collective invective about Jews, gays, African Americans, or any other minority group.) Mildly challenged by Alan Colmes, Fox News' in-house token "liberal" at the time, Coulter stuck by her guns:

COLMES: Would you like to convert these people [Muslims] all to Christianity?

COULTER: The ones that we haven't killed, yes.

COLMES: So no one should be Muslim. They should all be Christian?

COULTER: That would be a good start, yes . . .

The hate-mongering by the likes of Ann Coulter, Pat Robertson, and Franklin Graham has paved the way for the dangerous political rhetoric of the 2016 Republican presidential campaign. When it comes to Muslims or Arabs, a high-profile political personality like Donald Trump or Ben Carson can now say nearly anything that pops into his fevered brain without fear of any meaningful repercussions today. Following the November 2015 Paris terror attacks, Carson compared Muslims to rabid dogs and suggested, "If there's a rabid dog running around in your neighborhood, you're probably not going to assume something good about that dog." Carson did not have to spell out what people do with rabid dogs.

This anti-Muslim virulence has been building within US political circles for many years, of course, becoming particularly intense following 9/11. For example, at a November 2001 meeting with emergency responders in Valdosta, Georgia, then-Republican Congressman Saxby Chambliss remarked that we should "turn the sheriff loose and arrest every Muslim that crosses the state line." Even more frightening than the sheer lunacy of his statement was the fact that Chambliss was then chairman of the House Judiciary Subcommittee on Crime, Terrorism, and Homeland Security. Instead of voting him out of office the following November, the people of the great state of Georgia decided to elect Saxby Chambliss to the United State Senate.

Not to be outdone by Chambliss, then-Republican congressman John Cooksey from Louisiana, when asked about the concept of racial profiling during a radio interview, blurted out, "If I see someone that comes in that has a diaper on his head and a fan belt wrapped around the diaper on his head, that guy needs to be pulled over." Meanwhile—as President George W. Bush preached restraint, insisting that his war on terror was not a war on Islam—not everyone in his administration got the memo. In a November 2001 interview, devout church-goer Attorney General John Ashcroft declared, "Islam is a religion in which God requires you to send your son to die for him. . . . Christianity is a faith in which God sends his son to die for you."

It was Republican Congressman Peter King who turned Muslim hunting into an ongoing Capitol Hill crusade. Soon after taking over as chairman of the House Committee on Homeland Security in 2005, King decided to hold a high-profile congressional hearing— an investigation whose conclusions he signaled from the start by calling it "The Extent of Radicalization in the American Muslim Community and That Community's

Response." Like the anti-communist witchhunts of the Cold War, Congress was now announcing that it was once again legitimate to single out a segment of the American population whose belief system was considered suspect—in this case, religious beliefs embraced by millions of innocent Americans and protected under the First Amendment.

Congressman King has made little effort to conceal his anti-Islam bias, once publicly stating that "we have too many mosques in this country" and that extremists lead "80 to 85 percent of American mosques"—a wild and unfounded allegation that King pulled out of some dark part of his brain, or another part of his anatomy, to justify his demand for even more surveillance of the American Muslim community.

Scholarly studies of American Muslims have demonstrated how wrong King is, including a two-year joint study titled "Anti-Terror Lessons of Muslim-Americans," by Duke University professor David Schanzer and University of North Carolina professor Charles Kurzman, which found that American mosques are "actually a deterrent to the spread of militant Islam and terrorism." As Michael Leiter, President Barack Obama's former National Counterterrorism Center director, testified before King's own congressional panel in 2011, "Many of our tips to uncover active terrorist plots in the United States have come from the Muslim community."

As has been widely pointed out, there is a striking irony about Peter King's obsession with terrorism, since Congressman King himself was once a proud vocal supporter of the Irish Republican Army (IRA) when that group was officially designated a "terrorist" organization by the US State Department. King actively championed the IRA as a "legitimate force" fighting the British government and even helped raise funds for the militant group—support work that could have placed King in legal jeopardy under the anti-terror policies that he has strongly advocated in recent years.

"My problem with [King] is the hypocrisy," said Tom Parker, a counterterrorism specialist at Amnesty International who was once injured by an IRA bomb that struck a birthday party at a military hall in London in 1990. "If you say that terrorist violence is acceptable in one setting [like Ireland] because you happen to agree with the [IRA] cause, then you lose the authority to condemn it in another setting."

In the lead-up to King's anti-Muslim hearings, the spectacle of a congressional investigation specifically targeting a religious minority generated serious public concerns. "Rep. King's intent seems clear: To cast suspicion upon all Muslim Americans and to stoke the fires of anti-Muslim prejudice and Islamophobia," wrote Congressman Michael Honda (D-Calif.) in a February 2011 essay for the *San Francisco Chronicle*. Calling the congressional hearings a "sinister" ploy by King, Rep. Honda went on to say, "By framing his hearings as an investigation of the American Muslim community, the implication is that we should be suspicious of our Muslim neighbors, co-workers or classmates solely on the basis of their religion. This should be deeply troubling to Americans of all races and religions. An investigation specifically targeting a single religion implies, erroneously, a dangerous disloyalty, with one broad sweep of the discriminatory brush."

Rabbi Marc Schneier, president of the Foundation for Ethnic Understanding, was among the prominent interfaith leaders who took part in a large New York City rally in Times Square to protest King's congressional witchhunt. "To single out Muslim-Americans as the source of homegrown terrorism," Rabbi Schneier said, "and not examine all forms of violence motivated by extremist belief—that, my friends, is an injustice." Similarly, even prominent national security experts like Richard Clarke, the counterterrorism czar under both Presidents Bill Clinton and George W. Bush, warned that King's inquest would aid our enemies. "To the extent that these hearings make American Muslims feel that they are the object of fear-mongering, it will only serve Al Qaeda's ends," by wrongfully portraying that America is somehow at war with Islam, Clarke told *The Los Angeles Times*.

Former Congresswoman Michele Bachmann of Minnesota is another back-bencher who discovered she could extend her time in the political spotlight by demonizing Muslims. In Bachmann's deranged world, the United States is forever on the brink of being taken over by the falafel-eating, Mecca-praying, and Ramadan-fasting Muslim cabal of which I am a card-carrying member.

During her congressional tenure, Bachmann was a media fixture on cable news shows and right-wing talk radio, including Bryan Fischer's radio program. The American Family Association's Fischer is well known for his Islamophobic statements, which have included such unhinged statements as "the religious practice of Islam is not protected under the First Amendment," and "Muslims are stupid due to inbreeding." Fischer has advocated deporting Muslims from America and banning mosques in the United States.

In July 2012, Michelle Bachmann launched an outlandish witchhunt with four other conservative members of Congress aimed at then-Secretary of State Hillary Clinton's chief aide, Huma Abedin. Falsely charging that Abedin and her family had ties to Egypt's Muslim Brotherhood, Bachmann questioned whether Abedin was part of "a nefarious [Muslim] conspiracy to harm the United States by influencing US foreign policy with her high-level position at the State Department."

In a brave and uncommon move by a national Republican leader, Senator John McCain took to the US Senate floor to publicly and forcefully condemn Bachmann, defending Abedin as "an intelligent, upstanding, hard-working and loyal servant of our country and our government, who has devoted countless days of her life to advancing the ideals of the nation she loves and looking after its most precious interests. That she has done so while maintaining her characteristic decency, warmth and good humor is a testament to her ability to bear even the most arduous duties with poise and confidence . . . These sinister accusations rest solely on a few unspecified and unsubstantiated associations of members of Huma's family, none of which have been shown to harm or threaten the United States in any way. These attacks on Huma have no logic, no basis and no merit . . . And they need to stop now!"

"Put simply," McCain continued, "Huma represents what is best about America: the daughter of [Muslim] immigrants, who has risen to the highest levels of our government on the basis of her substantial personal merit and her abiding commitment to the American ideals that she embodies so fully. I am proud to know Huma and to call her my friend."

Huma Abedin, of course, is not the only US public official to be outrageously Muslim-baited. My dear friend Keith Ellison, the first American Muslim ever elected to Congress, was subjected to crude character assaults as soon as he won office in November 2006. Unsurprisingly, it was right-wing host Glenn Beck—a man who has built his career on afflicting the powerless and marginalized—who started Ellison's media lynching. "I have been nervous about this interview with you," Beck began, after Ellison graciously agreed to go on his show, "because what I feel like saying is, 'Sir, prove to me that you are not working with our enemies.'" Beck then added, "I'm not accusing you of being an enemy. . . . But that's the way I feel, and I think a lot of Americans will feel that way."

In fact, it was Ellison who should have been nervous going on Beck's show. For it was Glenn Beck who, just two months earlier, in September 2006, ominously warned that if "Muslims and Arabs" don't "act now . . . by step[ping] to the plate" to condemn terrorism, they would be "looking through a razor wire fence" from inside modern-day internment camps here in America.

Even political leaders who are lifelong Christians are not immune from Muslim-bashing, as President Obama himself can attest. Whenever I hear someone say, "Barack Obama is a Muslim," I feel like Jerry Seinfeld should jump out and say, "Not that there's anything wrong with that!" But Obama clearly has been made to feel that there *is* something wrong with that, after being consistently portrayed by Republicans as some sort of crypto-Muslim Manchurian Candidate. As a result of this right-wing, disinformation campaign, President Obama waited until his final year in office to visit an American mosque. To his credit, when he finally did address worshippers at the Islamic Society of Baltimore in February 2016, his message was strong and inspiring:

> "Let me say as clearly as I can as president of the United States: you fit right here. You're right where you belong. You're part of America too. You're not Muslim or American. You're Muslim and American."

Colin Powell tried to throw water on the growing "Obama is a Muslim" whisper campaign back during the 2008 presidential race when he stated forcefully on NBC's *Meet the Press* shortly before the election that he was "troubled" by the Republican efforts to disseminate the false rumor. "Well, the correct answer is . . . he is not a Muslim; he's a Christian. . . . He's always been a Christian." Powell then took another important step toward enlightening the American people when he added, "But the really right answer is . . . What if he is? Is there something wrong with being a Muslim in this country? The answer's no; that's not America. Is there something wrong with some seven-year-old

Muslim-American kid believing that he or she could be president?"

Powell's comments were well-intentioned, but they had little effect on the growing anti-Muslim intolerance in America. Nor did they even correct the false rumors about Obama. Even as late as September 2015, with Obama entering the final lap of his presidency, a joint CNN/ORC public opinion poll found that 29 percent of Americans and a staggering 43 percent of Republicans still believed that the man in the White House was a Muslim.

Among the leading purveyors of blatant falsehoods about Barack Obama is none other than Donald Trump, the real estate mogul and reality TV celebrity who emerged as an unlikely frontrunner in the 2016 GOP race. During a Trump rally in New Hampshire, one of the blowhard candidate's intellectually challenged supporters rose to his hind feet and delivered this remarkable statement into the microphone:

We have a problem in this country called Muslims. We know our current president is one [a Muslim]. You know he's not even an American. But anyway, we have training camps growing where they [Muslims] want to kill us. That's my question: When can we get rid of them [Muslims in America]?

Instead of challenging this blatantly racist and idiotic statement, Trump responded in equally moronic fashion:

> "We're going to be looking at a lot of different things and you know, a lot of people are saying that [Obama is a Muslim] and a lot of people are saying that bad things are happening and we're going to be looking at that and plenty of other things."

Unfortunately, the good and decent remarks about Muslims by prominent Americans like Colin Powell has been far outweighed in recent years by deliberately false and malicious rhetoric. This political demonization of Muslims has led to increasingly negative attitudes by Americans toward those US citizens who embrace Islam. In July 2014, a Zogby Analytics poll found that favorability in the United States toward Muslim Americans had dropped to 27 percent, from 36 percent in 2010. In the wake of the Paris and San Bernardino terror attacks blamed on ISIS, this anti-Muslim animus has only increased.

Polls show that negative feelings toward Muslims are particularly aggravated among Republicans. According to a September 2015 study, less than half of Iowa Republicans—49 percent—think the religion of Islam should even be legal in the United States, with only 38 percent of Trump supporters opposing the outlawing of Islam. These shocking statistics reveal an intolerance that has been granted rampant license by the poisonous speech of Republican Party leaders over the years.

So outlandish has Republican opinion about Muslims become that in December 2015, Public Policy Polling had a little fun by asking GOP voters if they supported bombing Agrabah, the fictional city in the Disney animated feature *Aladdin*. Nearly one-third of the Republicans polled responded *bombs away* on the Arabic-sounding city, even though it exists only in Disney's cartoon fantasia. Honestly, you don't know when to laugh or cry these days.

But Islamophobia is not just found on the right side of the political spectrum. It has also taken ugly root in some "liberal" circles as well. Stand-up comedian Bill Maher has turned his popular HBO show, *Real Time*, into a launch pad for anti-Islam hate missiles. Maher has called Islam the "one religion in the world that kills you when you disagree with them." (Tell that to the Planned Parenthood victims of evangelical Christian terrorist Robert Dear.) In his efforts to smear all Muslims as potential terrorists, Maher even once juxtaposed a picture of One Direction boy band member Zayn Malik—who happens to be Muslim—next to a photograph of the Boston Marathon bomber in order to get some cheap laughs.

Because we all look alike, right?

In September 2015, most of the civilized world rallied behind fourteen-year-old American Muslim teenager Ahmed Mohamed (aka "The Clock Boy") who was wrongfully arrested by Texas school officials for bringing one of his clock inventions to school to show his teachers. Even President Obama tried to make amends for the hurt and humiliation inflicted on the black Muslim kid by inviting Ahmed to the White House. But Maher would have none of this spirit of reconciliation—he lashed out at liberal "ninnies" (one of his favorite targets, next to Muslims) for supporting the teenaged inventor, insisting that the paranoid Texas officials "absolutely did the right thing, thinking it looked like a bomb."

"But it didn't look like a bomb; it looked like a clock," replied liberal commentator Ron Reagan, who was on Maher's guest panel that evening.

"It looked *exactly* like a bomb!" Maher barked back at him.

Bill Maher has also fretted out loud about the Islamic fertility rate in Western countries. "The most popular name in the United Kingdom, Great Britain—this was in the news this week—was Mohammed. Am I a racist to feel that I'm alarmed by that?"

Yeah, Bill, you are.

In October 2015, Maher hosted his fellow atheist (and anti-Muslim) comrade Richard Dawkins. At one point during the two men's anti-Muslim hate-fest, Dawkins dismissed the 1,400-year-old traditions and achievements of Islamic society; "To hell with their culture!" This is what passes for scholarly discussion of world religion on Maher's program.

As Maher fans know, the comedian—who is a militant atheist—has no fondness for any organized religion, which he feels spreads darkness and superstition throughout the world. But he reserves most of his spleen for Islam. By couching his prejudice as a defense of secular "liberal" values and sometimes sweetening his bitter pills with humor, Maher has made Muslim-bashing seem cooler than hate mongers like Franklin Graham or Ann Coulter (a favorite Maher guest) could ever make it. But the effect of Maher's anti-Muslim "comedy" routine is just the same as the rants from these raging bigots—it turns worshippers of Islam into a strange and suspect "other," into dangerous aliens unworthy of the respect and human rights that members of civilized white society deserve.

In response to the barrage of anti-Muslim invective from New Atheist polemicists like Bill Maher, world-renowned religious scholar Karen Armstrong— best-selling author of *A History of God*—stated that this poisonous rhetoric "fills me with despair . . . Because this is the sort of talk that led to the concentration camps in Europe. . . . This is the kind of thing people were saying about Jews in the 1930s and '40s in Europe."

Occasionally, Maher's Islam-smearing act becomes too much, even for the guests on his own show. In October 2014, actor Ben Affleck bravely challenged Maher's Islamophobia while appearing as a panelist on his show. The confrontation that evening began when Maher launched into a typical anti-Muslim harangue, comparing Islam to a "mafia" that will kill you if you say or draw the wrong thing. The TV host was no doubt emboldened that evening by the guest appearance of author Sam Harris, another "expert" Muslim-basher, though he has no expertise on Islam other than knowing he hates it. With Maher's encouragement, Harris began predictably venting his own hateful intolerance, calling Islam "the mother lode of bad ideas."

Usually, Maher's guests agree with rants like this or else squirm uncomfortably but silently. But to his great credit, Ben Affleck finally had enough that night, turning on Maher and Harris and challenging both of them for their "gross" and "racist" generalizations about Islam. With Affleck taking the lead, *New York Times* columnist Nicholas Kristof, another guest panelist that evening, was also inspired to take issue with Maher's indiscriminate and uninformed assault on Islam. Kristof noted that Maher's criticism of Islam has "a tinge of how white racists talk about African Americans and define blacks," with their sweeping racialized generalizations.

During another episode of *Real Time*, in April 2015, CNN host Fareed Zakaria also challenged Maher's increasingly virulent bigotry. Zakaria suggested that Maher had become so completely addicted to the punchline value of his anti-Muslim routine, even though it produced no public understanding whatsoever. "You're going to make a lot of news for yourself, and get a lot of applause lines and joke lines," Zakaria scolded Maher, adding that he would never help effect change by insulting an entire religion. Zakaria added that Maher should show "some sense of respect," since he was talking about the second-largest religion in the world. Thrown off-balance by Fareed Zakaria's critique—who is clearly Maher's intellectual superior when it comes to understanding the history of Islam and the interplay of religion and politics on the global stage—the TV host could only childishly snap that he found his guest's criticism "insulting." For a man who has built a career on insulting others, Bill Maher is surprisingly thin-skinned himself.

As TV and radio hosts gave voice to the ugliest sentiments in the American psyche and as political leaders jostled to exploit these base passions, some leaders spoke out in dismay. Speaking with Jake Tapper of CNN, former Republican presidential candidate John McCain commented darkly on the Islamophobic rhetoric of the 2016 GOP campaign. "I think we are hurting ourselves," said Senator McCain. "If we disparage . . . and impugn the character of [fellow Americans who happen to be Muslim] . . . then obviously there's a trust and support deficit amongst the American people." Senator McCain finished his CNN interview by stating, "I'm afraid we will pay a price at the polls."

There should indeed be a political price for scapegoating millions of people simply because of their religious faith. But, unfortunately, McCain is probably wrong. Even the most wild and deranged assertions about Islamic believers will continue to go largely unpunished by voters, because after years of anti-Muslim defamation in the US media, hating and fearing Arabs, Muslims, and South Asians has become the new normal. These days, everyone knows that you can say whatever you want about Islam and Muslims in the public domain with complete impunity.

Chapter Three

The Sharia Bogeyman

There is still some debate as to when the term "Islamophobia" was officially introduced into our global lexicon. Many people point to the use of the term by the Runnymede Trust, Britain's leading multiculturalism think tank, in a report titled *Islamophobia: A Challenge for Us All* that was released in November 1997 by then-British Home Secretary Jack Straw. But according to Robin Richardson, who edited the Runnymede report, the term "Islamophobia" was actually much older than the think tank's 1997 report. Richardson traced the term to early twentieth-century critiques of the French term *Islamophobie* in regard to the treatment of Muslim colonized subjects by French administrators.

The first known use in print of the French term *Islamophobie* appears to have been in a 1910 book published in Paris titled *La Politique Musulmane Dans l'Afrique Occidentale Française,* by Alain Quellien, a scholarly critique of French policy toward the colonized peoples of West Africa. The first printed use of the word "Islamophobia" in the English language appears to have been made in an 1985 article by the late Palestinian academic giant Edward Said, when he referred in passing to "the connection . . . between Islamophobia and anti-Semitism." Professor Said criticized writers who did not recognize that "hostility to Islam in the modern Christian West has historically gone hand-in-hand" with anti-Semitism and that this hatred of Islam "has stemmed from the same source and been nourished at the same stream" of xenophobia.

The next recorded use of the word in English was in the American journal *Insight* in February 1991 in reference to the hostility of the Russian government toward its own Muslim citizens and regions. "Islamophobia also accounts for Moscow's reluctance to relinquish its position in Afghanistan, despite the estimated $300 million a month it takes to keep the Kabul regime going," wrote author Nathan Lean. He went on to note that "in its earliest historical usage, the term 'Islamophobia' described prejudice and hostility towards Muslims—not an 'irrational fear of Islam.'" But these days, it all seems of the same poisonous bundle—the irrational fear of Islam, as well as the bias and hate crimes that go along with it.

At the heart of Islamophobia lies a dark ignorance, wrote Reza Aslan in a 2014 article in *The Atlantic* about the term itself. "As with any kind of bigotry, anti-Muslim sentiment is not based on a rational response but an emotional one. Bigotry is a result of fear. Speaking about it as a phobia makes sense. . . . Bigotry resides in the heart, not brain. . . . The problem with an emotional response like fear is that it is impervious to data and information. I would say that all racism and bigotry is '-phobic' in one sense or the other."

Freedom of religion, of course, is protected under the US Constitution, a deeply held cultural value that has made America a hospitable home for millions of native-born Muslims as well as immigrants and refugees from Islamic countries; and an inhospitable home for millions of black African Muslims who were brought over here on slave ships centuries before Donald Trump's immigrant ancestors arrived here from Germany. But with rising intolerance in recent years, many American Muslims no longer feel welcome in their own country. According to a study titled "The Impact of the September 11 Attacks on Arab and Muslim Communities in the United States," by Louise Cainkar, a sociology professor at Marquette University, by 2004 at least 100,000 Muslim Americans living in the United States had suffered one of the authoritarian measures adopted after 9/11, including arbitrary arrest, secret and prolonged detention, closed hearing, government snooping on privileged attorney-client conversations, wiretapping, and compulsory special registration.

In addition, harassment of Islamic worshippers throughout the country has become so severe that many fear for their physical safety. In Bridgeport, Connecticut, American Muslim community leaders had to eventually ask local police and elected officials for increased security so that they could worship in peace after an angry mob protested outside their local mosque. According to reports, about a dozen members of a North Carolina–based fundamentalist Christian group self-righteously calling itself "Operation Save America" confronted peaceful worshippers at the Masjid An-Noor mosque in Bridgeport and yelled what mosque members described as "hate-filled slogans" against Muslims seeking to worship in peace.

In November 2015, as the madness in the air continued to grow, a mosque in the Dallas suburb of Irving became the target of a similar demonstration. But this time, in a brazen display of intimidation, some of the protesters carried guns, including at least one assault rifle and shotgun. The group further invited violence by also posting on Facebook the names and addresses of local Muslims and what they termed "Muslim sypmathizers."

These public displays of hatred and firepower are part of a nationwide terror campaign directed at mosques and Islamic community centers, under the obscenely misnamed banner "Global Rally for Humanity." Can you imagine what would happen if the members of any other religious group in America were forced to walk past a phalanx of belligerent "patriots"—many of them heavily armed—simply so they could gather in their house of worship? As *The Dallas Morning News* commented after the Irving protest, "The outcry would be loud and long." If gun-toting American Muslims ever showed up outside a white church, Fox News's Bill O'Reilly and Sean Hannity would call for the heavens to rain fire.

One of the organizers of this anti-Muslim campaign is a former US Marine (and self-proclaimed Oath Keeper) named Jon Ritzheimer, who gained a degree of notoriety in 2015 for coordinating an anti-mosque protest in Phoenix that drew hundreds of armed protesters. At another rally the same year, he proudly sold black "FUCK ISLAM" T-shirts. He also once bizarrely threatened to arrest Senator Debbie Stabenow of Michigan for "treason" because she supported President Obama's nuclear deal with Iran.

Ritzheimer again demonstrated his knack for publicity when he popped up among the anti-government militants who seized control of a federal park building on an Oregon wildlife refuge in December 2015.

While the gun-toting firebrands get most of the headlines, the anti-mosque campaign also has been embraced by politicians across the country. As Professor John Esposito, founding director of the Alwaleed bin Talal Center for Christian-Muslim Understanding at Georgetown University, has observed, "Especially troubling is the fact that [anti-mosque] protesters were not simply uneducated or marginalized bigots, neo-con media and political commentators, and hardline Christian pastors, but also American politicians who belonged to mainstream political parties, [including] aspiring presidential candidates, members of Congress and other political candidates as well."

In July 2012, for example, Colorado Republican state senator Kevin Grantham hosted the notorious Dutch anti-Muslim politician Geert Wilders, who brought to America his message that new mosques must be banned. Grantham freely vented his prejudice to *The Colorado Statesman*, telling the newspaper, "Mosques are not churches like we would think of churches. [Muslims] think of mosques more as a foothold into a society, as a foothold into a community, more in the cultural and in the nationalistic sense. Our churches—we don't feel that way, they're places of worship, and mosques are simply not that and we need to take that into account when approving construction [of new American mosques]."

Again, what would Fox News—or *The New York Times*, for that matter—do if a public official loudly called for blocking the construction of new churches or synagogues in America? But Grantham's ugly crusade brought him no vehement public censure. "Where's the outrage?" wondered *Colorado Pols*, the state politics blog. Clearly this sort of outrageous Muslim-bashing has simply become the new political norm. Even though every responsible official from President Obama on down will tell you that American mosques are over-whelmingly calming influences in the lives of everyday Muslims, there is no arguing with hate-mongers like Grantham and Wilders.

Anti-Muslim hysteria has a dark and wild life of its own, flapping its wings frantically across the country without ever touching down in reality. Nothing exem-plifies the current mad flight of Islamophobia more than the absurd tempest over Sharia (Islamic law). To listen to this debate sweeping the land is truly to get lost in the mad screeching of birds.

Any red-blooded American with an eighth-grade education knows that our Supremacy Clause clearly states that "the Constitution and the laws of the United States [are] the supreme law of the land"—which means that no other law in the world (either foreign or domes-tic) can trump it.

Nope, not even Sharia law.

Yet, in direct defiance of reality, an entire conservative cottage industry has developed in the United States dedicated to spreading the lunatic idea that traditional Islamic law is about to replace the American way of life. This fear campaign has somehow succeeded in persuading legislators in more than thirty American states to introduce anti-Sharia legislation. While they're at it, why don't these legislators take action to make sure that Arabic doesn't become the official language of the US of A or pass laws to prevent camel racing from replacing the Kentucky Derby?

Right-wing fear mongers know that the Sharia conspiracy theory is a scam. But they clearly see it as a major political wedge issue, one that can be used to exploit public anxieties during the endless war on terror. "Anti-Sharia law initiatives [might] be in future election cycles what anti-gay marriage initiatives were before," Marc Ambinder of *The Atlantic* once speculated. "That is, a cultural wedge issue the [Republican Party] uses to ensure that hard-core conservatives enthusiastically flock to the polls."

The only real Republican pushback against the Sharia scare strategy came from New Jersey Governor Chris Christie a few years ago. In August 2011, Governor Christie appointed a Muslim-American lawyer named Sohail Mohammed to a state judicial bench, which immediately ruffled some feathers among right-wing anti-Sharia circles. When asked about these concerns, Christie made it clear that he had no patience for such blatant Islamophobia. "Ignorance is behind the criticism of Sohail Mohammed," Christie stated during a press conference, adding that he was "disgusted—candidly—by some of the questions" that he had been asked at Mohammed's confirmation hearings. This "Sharia law business is just crap . . . and I'm tired of dealing with the crazies." Mohammed had become a target "just because of his religious background," concluded Christie.

Unfortunately, this moral courage deserted Christie during the increasingly wacky 2016 Republican presidential race. Trailing far behind the GOP pack, the New Jersey governor tried to light a fire under his campaign by joining in the anti-Muslim frenzy of the Republican frontrunners. Christie took an extreme stand against Syrian refugees, stating that none of these desperate souls should be given sanctuary in America, not even "orphans under five," as he told a radio show in 2015.

Former Republican presidential candidate Newt Gingrich got the Sharia scam rolling during his short-lived bid for the 2012 GOP presidential nomination. Calling Sharia a "mortal threat to the survival of freedom in the United States"—*huh?*—Gingrich boldly declared his opposition "to any efforts to impose Sharia in the United States," as if robed mullahs were already gathering ominously on the steps of the US Capitol.

Furthermore, Newt announced, "We should have a federal law that says under no circumstances in any jurisdiction in the United States will Sharia [law] be used in any court to apply to any judgment made about American law."

Even more bizarrely, Gingrich also proceeded to suggest that the Supreme Court had somehow become an Islamist sleeper cell, accusing Justices Stephen Breyer and Elena Kagan of insufficient vigilance, and stating that "no judge [should] remain in office who tries to use Sharia law to interpret the United States Constitution."

Gingrich's asinine statements received thunderous applause from the conservative faithful, a crowd that—as usual—proved blithely unperturbed by the fact that one of its leaders was utterly disconnected from reality.

By the way, Gingrich was among those prominent figures on the right who later expressed at least qualified support for Donald Trump's stunning proposal to ban Muslims from the United States. Trump's inflammatory suggestion was condemned by government leaders around the world and even by some prominent members of his own unhinged party, like presidential rival Jeb Bush, who called Trump's idea, well, "unhinged" (while a Bush aide labeled it, with equal accuracy, "fascistic").

But Bush had demeaned himself just days earlier by calling for a religious screen test for admitting Syrian refugees into the country, insisting that our national

compassion be limited only to Christians. And meanwhile, a number of other leading conservatives rushed
to Trump's support, including commentator Laura
Ingraham, who tweeted, "Anyone who thinks [Trump's]
comments will hurt him don't know the temperature of
the American ppl."

The outbreak of hateful Trump mania in the
Republican Party was made possible by years of bigotry campaigns like the anti-Sharia crusade. To give you
some sense of how detached that anti-Sharia crazies are
from reality, just ponder these numbers. We American
Muslims currently represent less than 2 percent of the
American population and there are only two Muslims
who currently serve in the United States Congress—
Democratic congressmen Keith Ellison of Minnesota
and Andre Carson of Indiana. There are no Muslims in
President Obama's cabinet, none on the Supreme Court
bench, and none serving as state governors. Despite
Muslims' all but invisible presence in political leader-
ship circles, from the ear-splitting outcry over "Sharia
tyranny," one would think that the Senate cafeteria had
begun serving only falafels and couscous and those legendary smoke-filled rooms now feature olive-skinned,
bearded politicians puffing on hookahs.

While the conservative fear campaign is completely
disconnected from reality, it nonetheless is clearly
working. For instance, a 2011 public opinion poll by

the Public Religion Research Institute showed that 30 percent of Americans believe Muslims want to establish Sharia law within the United States. (Unsurprisingly, the percentage was even higher—52 percent—among those who said they rely on the Fox News Channel as their primary source of news.)

"The suggestion that Sharia threatens American security is disturbingly reminiscent of the accusation, in nineteenth-century Europe, that Jewish religious law was seditious," Yale University Professor Eliyahu Stern wrote in an opinion piece for *The New York Times* bluntly titled "Don't Fear Islamic Law in America."

Fear that Jewish law bred disloyalty was not limited to political elites; leading European philosophers also entertained the idea. [German philosopher Immanuel] Kant argued that the particularistic nature of "Jewish legislation" made Jews "hostile to all other peoples." And [fellow German philosopher Georg] Hegel contended that Jewish dietary rules and other Mosaic laws barred Jews from identifying with their fellow Prussians and called into question their ability to be civil servants . . . Most Americans today would be appalled if Muslims suffered from legally sanctioned discrimination as Jews once did in Europe.

Still, there are signs that many Americans view Muslims in this country as disloyal.

Just like past generations of xenophobic fear-mongers who tried to paint Jewish law (known as Halacha in Hebrew) in a sinister light, these modern-day peddlers of hate are attempting to do the same with Muslims today, exploiting most Americans' ignorance about Islam as well as the public's limited understanding of the country's constitutional laws and guiding principles.

"In fact, for most of its history, Islamic law offered the most liberal and humane legal principles available anywhere in the world," Harvard Law Professor Noah Feldman noted in a *New York Times Magazine* article.

One reason for the divergence between Western and Muslim views of Sharia is that we are not all using the word to mean the same thing. Although it is commonplace to use the word "Sharia" and the phrase "Islamic law" interchangeably . . . in fact, "Sharia" is not the word traditionally used in Arabic to refer to the processes of Islamic legal reasoning or the rulings produced through it: that word is fiqh, meaning something like Islamic jurisprudence . . . Westerners typically imagine that Sharia advocates simply want to use the Quran as their legal code. But the reality is much more complicated.

First of all, it should be noted that any mainstream religious scholar of Islam will tell you that there is no single monolithic definition of Sharia as it exists today anywhere in the world. Very generally speaking, the concept of Sharia has come to be defined as "the ideal law of God according to Islamic tradition," stated Professor Intisar Rabb, director of the Islamic Legal Studies Program at Harvard Law School. But, as Rabb made clear, "Sharia has tremendous diversity, as jurists and learned scholars figure out and articulate what that law is [for the twenty-first century]. Historically, Sharia served as a means for political dissent against arbitrary rule. It is not a monolithic doctrine of violence, as has been characterized in the recently introduced [anti-Sharia] bills that would criminalize [basic Islamic] practices" like charity giving and other benign legal matters like divorce and estate planning.

"Some of the biggest misperceptions about Islamic law are that it proposes a scheme of global domination," said Imam Zaid Shakir, a cofounder of Zaytuna College in Berkeley, California—the first Muslim liberal arts college in America—during an interview for this book. He also noted that many Westerners mistakenly believe that Islamic law "is not amenable to change in the face of changing circumstances, that it is a system that oppresses women . . . and that by definition, it is an enemy of western civilization." In fact, continued Imam

Shakir, Islamic law actually forbids many of the practices that the average person fearfully associates with Muslims today.

"For example, Sharia forbids members of a Muslim minority [in Western societies] from engaging in clandestine acts of violence and paramilitary organizing . . . or from acting as political or military agents for a Muslim-majority country," the imam told me. "Islamic law also forbids the disruption of public safety." All this would certainly come as a surprise to the many people who know little about Islam—whether they are extremists who profess to be devout Muslims or those who seek to politically exploit anti-Muslim fear and ignorance

Lost in all the sound and fury about Sharia is another very crucial fact: Sharia only applies to observant Muslims, in the same way that the Halacha, traditional Jewish law, only applies to the observant Jews who choose to follow it. Sharia does not apply in any way whatsoever to non-Muslims. Echoing Professor Stern of Yale, Professor Rabb noted that Sharia "historically was a broad system that encompassed ritual laws, so in some ways it recalls Jewish law that has rules for how to pray, how to make ablution before prayers" as well as dietary rules involving kosher (or halal) food.

As Stern pointed out, current anti-Sharia efforts would not only interfere with Muslims' ability to lead their personal lives according to their religious principles but "would go even further in stigmatizing Islamic life" in America. By way of illustration, he pointed to legislation introduced in the Tennessee General Assembly that would equate Sharia with the very destruction of the United States.

Political observers point out that our country has a long, raucous history of witch hunts. "In times of economic distress, people tend to be more susceptible to charlatans and demagogues telling them who to blame and who to fear," Matthew Duss, former national security editor at the Center for American Progress, once told me for a magazine article that I once wrote on this topic. "America has been through this sort of thing before with various minority groups, but we've always come through it stronger in the end. . . . Hopefully within a few years, the idea that all American Muslims want to turn America into an Islamic state will seem as stupid as the idea that a Catholic president would take orders from the Vatican."

But in the meantime, America must sweat through a raging fever, a blaze of intolerance that puts many Muslim citizens at risk of losing their rights and, in some cases, their lives. Fear and ignorance, of course, fuel this anti-Muslim hysteria. But so does money. Because there is political capital in scapegoating Muslims.

In order to truly understand the growth of the anti-Sharia movement in the United States today—and the rise of Islamophobia in general—it is important to understand that there are literally millions of dollars that are flowing from right-wing funders to some of the leading Islam bashers. According to a 2011 Center for American Progress report titled "Fear Inc.: The Roots of the Islamophobia Network in America," during the past decade, seven well-endowed American foundations and individual donors have provided over $42 million dollars to some of the most dangerous anti-Muslim activists. These funders of hate include the Donors Capital Fund, Richard Mellon Scaife Foundation, Lynde and Harry Bradley Foundation, Newton and Rochelle Becker Foundation/Charitable Trust, Russell Berrie Foundation, Anchorage Charitable Fun, and Fairbrook Foundation. The lion's share of this hate funding went to anti-Muslim activists such as Frank Gaffney (Center for Security Policy), David Yerushalmi (Society of Americans for National Existence, the American Freedom Law Center), Daniel Pipes (Middle East Forum), Robert Spencer (Jihad Watch), and Steven Emerson (The Investigative Project).

According to the "Fear Inc." report, David Yerushalmi and anti-Muslim zealot Pamela Geller have been two of the most outspoken (and successful) advocates for anti-Sharia legislation over the years. Due to the efforts of militant activists like Yerushalmi and Geller, stated the report, by 2015 at least thirty-two states had either introduced or passed legislation to ban the nonexistent threat of Sharia law in their courtrooms.

It was Yerushalmi's right-wing think tank, the Society of Americans for National Existence, that first proposed legislation in 2007 to make adherence to Sharia "a felony punishable by up to 20 years in prison." According to a report by the Anti-Defamation League (ADL), Yerushalmi has a "record of anti-Muslim, anti-immigrant and anti-black bigotry." Writing in the *Middle East Quarterly* in 2011, Yerushalmi insisted that "The Mythical 'moderate' Muslim ... the Muslim who embraces traditional Islam but wants a peaceful coexistence with the West, is effectively non-existent." He has argued that the war on terror should be a war on Islam and on "all Muslim Americans" and has advocated deporting Muslim-Americans and other "non-Western, non-Christian" people to protect America's "national character."

In addition, Yerushalmi has ranted against "progressive elites" and even once called African Americans "the most murderous of peoples" in the past as well. The Southern Poverty Law Center has designated Yerushalmi's organization as a "hate group." Yerushalmi is closely aligned in the anti-Sharia movement with the flamboyant anti-Muslim activist Pamela Geller. According to the Anti-Defamation League, Geller presents "herself as an expert on Islam, promoting the theory that there is an Islamic conspiracy to destroy American values and culture." The ADL further stated that "much of her pseudo-expertise on Islam is built on exploiting public fears of a grand Muslim con spiracy that will reach every neighborhood across the country if left unchecked." The Southern Poverty Law Center, which also lists Geller's organization (the American Freedom Defense Initiative) as a hate group, noted that the former New York journalist "has seized the role of the anti-Muslim movement's most visible and influential figurehead. Her strengths are panache and vivid rhetorical flourishes—not to mention stunts like posing for an anti Muslim video in a bikini." The Southern Poverty Law Center further states that Geller is prone to publicizing preposterous claims, such as that President Obama is the "love child of Malcolm X" and that Supreme Court Justice Elena Kagan, who is Jewish, "supports Nazi ideology." Geller herself, added the law center, has "mingled with European racists and fascists, spoken favorably of South African racists and defended Serbian war criminal Slobodan Milosevic" in the past.

Back in December 2011, I debated Pamela Geller on Dr. Drew Pinsky's CNN *Headline News* show. The topic was the short-lived TLC reality television show *All-American Muslim*, which lost its two prominent corporate sponsors—Lowe's Home Improvement and Kayak.com—after the advertisers buckled in the face of an anti-Muslim campaign. I, of course, was outraged by this rank display of corporate cowardice. By featuring such real-life characters as a Wayne County, Michigan, federal agent, high school football coach, and sheriff's deputy—all of whom were born into the Islamic faith—*All-American Muslim* followed in the path of numerous reality shows, sitcoms, and dramas depicting other minorities (including blacks, Latinos, Jews, and gays) as part of the everyday American fabric. But this was clearly too much for hate-mongers like Geller, who defended the sabotaging of the show during our debate.

The letter-writing campaign that succeeded in stampeding Lowe's and Kayak was organized by a self-proclaimed Christian group in the sunshine state called the Florida Family Association. The Tampa-based organization had urged the companies to pull their ads from *All-American Muslim* because the show was a "propaganda [vehicle] clearly designed to counter legitimate and present-day concerns about many Muslims who are advancing Islamic fundamentalism and Sharia law." Of course, this argument was the sophomoric equivalent of saying that the popular TLC reality show *Sister Wives* was really an insidious secret campaign to promote fundamentalist Mormon polygamy across America.

By way of explaining its spineless decision, Lowe's issued a weak statement on its Facebook page, stating that *All-American Muslims* had become a "lightning rod . . . on this topic." What topic? Islam? Patriotic American Muslims? Right-wing intolerance? Lowe's didn't specify, simply concluding, "As a result, we did pull our advertising on this program."

Now, what made this national controversy even more troubling was the more than twelve thousand comments responding to Lowe's Facebook statement, the great volume of which endorsed the hardware giant's decision—and in racist, jingoistic language that was a lot less oblique than Lowe's. Here's a sampling of the comments on Lowe's page:

- "Thank you Lowes, for pulling your advertising from "All American Muslims" show (there is no such thing as "All American Muslims")"
- "[The women on the TLC show] were almost pretty, till they put rags on their heads."
- "How dare these people come into our country and try to take over and push their religion onto us!"
- "Thank you for pulling your support for American Muslim [sic], now I will come back and shop in your stores."

Almost exactly one year later, in late 2012, Pamela Geller took her Islamophobia to new heights (or new lows) when she purchased prominent advertising space in several New York City subway stations to display her newest anti-Islam message. According to *The New York Observer*, Geller's belligerent ads featured a "panorama of the sky the moment the World Trade Center burst into flames [on September 11], accompanied by a quote from the Quran that reads 'Soon shall We cast terror into the hearts of the Unbelievers.'"

Imagine how millions of peace-loving Christians would react if they saw subway advertisements during their morning commute showing the bombed-out ruins and carnage left by a US drone strike in Pakistan or Yemen, along with cherry-picked, out-of-context Bible verses such as "I come not to bring peace, but a sword" (Matthew 10:34) or "I have come to cast fire upon the earth; and how I wish it were already kindled" (Luke 12:49-51), trying to wrongfully portray Christianity as a religion of violence. I think that it would be fair to say that most fair-minded Americans would be able to see right through the sinister veneer of these blatantly anti-Christian advertisements.

In response to those who think that Islam is more of an inherently violent religion than any other world faith, Professor Philip Jenkins, codirector of the Historical Studies on Religion program at Baylor University, once provided some illuminating context during a 2010 interview with NPR. "By the standards of the time, which is the seventh century A.D., the laws of war that are laid down by the Quran are actually reasonably humane," Professor Jenkins told millions of NPR listeners. "Then we turn to the Bible, and we actually find something that is for many people a real surprise. There is a specific kind of warfare laid down in the Bible which we can only call genocide. . . . Much to my surprise, the Islamic scriptures in the Quran were actually far less bloody and less violent than those in the Bible."

Regardless of the violent messages that can be extracted from the Bible, as well as the Quran, nobody should be in the business of cherry-picking religious texts to promote intolerance within our respective societies. All of the great religions of the world feature holy scripture and teachings that promote peace, compassion, and human understanding. These are the shining words that must light our way forward, as the peoples of the world struggle to embrace love, not hate.

Chapter Four

White Terror

On July 22, 2011, the Scandinavian nation of Norway was rocked by the worst terrorist attack the country had ever endured when a massive car explosion shook the center of the capital, Oslo. The blast blew out the windows of the prime minister's offices and damaged the finance and oil ministry buildings as well. Eight people were killed and over two hundred injured in the first attack, leaving a scene of carnage that witnesses described as "a war zone."

But the mayhem had just begun.

About ninety minutes later, a young blond-haired man in a police uniform was transported via ferry to the island of Utøya, located in a lake about twenty-four miles northwest of Oslo. The man, who was armed with a pistol and an automatic rifle, was the terrorist who had just planted the car bomb. And he was about to continue his bloody spree, which would later be called one of "the worst terrorist atrocities in Europe since World War II."

When the thirty-two-year-old terrorist—a self-proclaimed "modern-day crusader" against Islam and multiculturalist values named Anders Breivik—arrived on the island of Utøya, he immediately started shooting indiscriminately at hundreds of young Norwegian teenagers who were attending a Labour Party youth camp. In his police uniform, Breivik was able to lure many of the teenagers toward him, with cries of "You're safe!" before mowing them down in a shower of bullets. Many of the teenagers threw themselves into the freezing waters of the surrounding lake in an attempt to escape the carnage. Breivik did not stop his butchery until he finally ran out of bullets, at which point he quietly surrendered himself to the arriving SWAT team. His rampage that day—during which he maniacally laughed and yelled, "You all must die!"—would leave seventy-seven teenagers dead and more than one hundred others wounded.

According to a Norwegian judge and Breivik's attorney, the Norwegian "crusader" promptly acknowledged carrying out the "gruesome but necessary" attacks, explaining they were aimed at preventing the "colonization" of the country by Muslims and accusing the liberal Labour Party of "treason" for promoting multiculturalism in Norway and welcoming Muslim immigrants. Investigators soon located a sprawling manifesto extending over 1,500 pages that Breivik had cobbled together from numerous sources, including the work of American Islamophobes like the aforementioned Pamela Geller and Daniel Pipes. The Norwegian "crusader's" lengthy rant, titled "2083—A European Declaration of Independence," inveighed against the "Islam-ification of Europe" and the Labour Party's "cultural Marxist/multiculturalist ideals," and included meticulous plans for attacking his enemies. The digital manifesto also included photographs of Breivik wearing a customized US Marine Corps dress jacket with medals of the Knights Templar—an order of Christian crusaders who fought against Muslim rule of the Holy Land in the Middle Ages.

As soon as news of the shocking mass murder in Norway broke, the US media was filled with speculation that it was the work of Muslim terrorists. This was the same rush to judgment that had occurred after the 1995 bombing of the Oklahoma City federal building when "Middle Eastern–looking men" were blamed for the attack that turned out to have been masterminded by an anti government, white terrorist named Timothy McVeigh. Among the media outlets prematurely suggesting a jihadist connection to the Norway massacre were *The New York Times* and *The Washington Post*.

Unsurprisingly, right-wing pundit Laura Ingraham also rushed to pin the crime on Muslims while guest hosting the Fox News channel's *The O'Reilly Factor* on the evening of the Breivik atrocity—even though by the time Ingraham went on air, news reports were already circulating that the suspect in custody was a white European who espoused an extremist Christian ideology. But this didn't stop Fox from immediately seeking to criminalize Muslims. After all, this is a network run by Roger Ailes, a conservative propagandist who, according to a 2011 profile in *Rolling Stone* magazine, "has a personal paranoia about people who are Muslim."

As you can probably imagine, Pamela Geller—America's favorite, camera-loving Islamophobe—also wasted no time in blaming Muslims for the Norway terrorist attacks. "Jihad in Norway?" Geller wrote on her website soon after the news of the attacks started to break. Shortly after, she posted a second item, stating, "You cannot avoid the consequences of ignoring jihad," while linking to a previous blog item that she had bluntly headlined "Norway: ALL Rapes in Past 5 Years Committed by Muslims."

Then, as William Saletan later wrote in *Slate*, "things went horribly wrong [for Pamela Geller]. It turned out that the suspected terrorist in Norway wasn't a Muslim. He hated Muslims. . . . And he admired Geller."

As Saletan pointed out, the self-proclaimed "cultural Christian" terrorist praised Pamela Geller numerous times throughout his crazed manifesto, citing her blog more than 250 times.

"Now you know how it feels, Miss Geller," continued Saletan, "when the terrorist is a Christian . . . and when the preacher to whom he has been linked is you. . . . You suddenly discover the injustice of group blame and guilt-by-association."

In fact, as it turned out, Anders Breivik drew inspiration for his depraved murder spree from a variety of notorious figures in the American Islamophobia network, including Pamela Geller, Robert Spencer, and Daniel Pipes. *The New York Times* found that Breivik's manifesto quoted Spencer alone at least sixty-four times. Commenting on professional Muslim-haters like Gellers and Spencer, former CIA officer Mark Sagemen remarked, "They and their [anti-Muslim] writings are the infrastructure from which Breivik emerged. This rhetoric . . . is not cost-free."

As Professor Matthew Goodwin, an expert on right-wing extremism at the University of Nottingham in England, pointed out, ironically Breivik was radicalized by the same online process as many of the jihadists that he so loathed. In this sense, Breivik should not be simply dismissed as "insane" or a "lone wolf," as he was by much of the media. In truth, he is part of a network of young, militant white supremacists throughout Europe who ingest the same hate propaganda that galvanized him to commit his reign of terror. British journalist Nick Lowles noted that "Somewhere, in a front room or bedroom, other young [white Christian extremist] men are probably dreaming up fantasies about saving western civilization from the evils of communism and Islam. . . . We ignore what motivated Breivik at our peril."

The Breivik nightmare, of course, is not simply a European phenomenon. Shifting our focus back to our own American shores, there have been several high-profile acts of mass murder that would have certainly been labeled "terrorism" if the perpetrators had been brown-skinned Arab or Muslim men with foreign-sounding names. In March 2010, a thirty-six-year-old, white computer programmer from California named John Patrick Bedell walked up to two security guards outside the Pentagon Metro station in suburban Washington, D.C., and started shooting at them with a semiautomatic pistol. The guards, who were lightly injured, returned fire, fatally wounding Bedell. The gunman was later identified as a libertarian with strong anti-government views.

Just the previous month, another anti-government white terrorist named Andrew "Joe" Stack flew his single-engine airplane into an Internal Revenue Service (IRS) building in Austin, Texas, killing an IRS manager and himself and injuring thirteen others. Stack left behind a suicide letter in which he detailed his grievances against a federal tax system that he believed was weighted heavily in favor of corporate interests and against average Americans like himself. "Desperate times call for desperate measures," Stack chillingly explained.

While the Bedell and Stack actions were clearly designed for dramatic effect, many other violent acts of apparently political nature go largely unnoticed in the United States, where the bar for media attention has been set at a high body count. According to the Southern Poverty Law Center, our country has been experiencing an "explosive growth in extremist-group activism across the United States" in recent years. The law center reported that so-called "patriot groups"— right-wing outfits steeped in anti-government conspiracy theories—grew in number from 149 in 2008 to 512 in 2009—an astonishing 244 percent increase that apparently reflected a backlash against the election of America's first African American president.

Of course, if any of these largely overlooked acts of anti-government violence had been committed by someone with a Muslim-sounding name like Aziz Ansari (my apologies to the stand-up comedian), instead of white dudes with forgettable names like John Bedell and Joe Stack, you can bet your bottom dollar they would have gotten the full media-spotlight treatment, including frenzied round-the-clock cable commentary, packs of journalists busting through police tape into suspects' apartments, and national security experts screaming for more missile barrages and boots on the ground. The whole nine yards. I mean, just *imagine* if a shooter packing two semiautomatics started blasting away in the Pentagon Metro station ... and he turned out to be named something like Aziz Ansari. Donald Trump's already fiery orange hair (or whatever the hell that is) would have instantly burst into flame.

Or let's imagine that we all woke up on a beautiful summer morning to hear the breaking news of a bearded, brown-skinned, gun-toting fanatic who stormed into a Wisconsin church full of innocent white people and then brutally murdered six innocent congregants in cold-blood while they prayed at their house of worship. If a scenario like that occurred, few Americans would have any problem seeing it as an act of "terrorism"—and the media circus would instantly reflect that assessment.

In real life, something like that did happen, but with an important difference. The actual shooter was a forty-year-old white supremacist named Wade Michael Page and the innocent murder victims were bearded, brown men and foreign-looking women wearing head coverings. In this all-too real case, the media was not so sure it was an act of terrorism. But that's precisely what it was.

The house of worship that Page burst into on that bright Sunday morning in August 2012 was a Sikh temple. Afterward, one of the congregation's stunned members told a local news station, "Nobody's angry here. We're just confused. . . . Was this directed at us because of the way we look?"

Sadly, the short answer is yes.

Since observant Sikh men wear a turban (known as a "dastaar" or "pagri") and also keep long unshorn beards as part of their faith, many Americans after September 11 wrongfully conflated Sikh Americans with Muslims, our society's new pariahs. In fact, as if to highlight the sheer tragic irony and flat out human ignorance of bias-motivated crimes, the first victim of a post-9/11 hate crime murder in the United States was neither a Muslim nor an Arab but a Sikh—a forty-nine-year-old Indian-American businessman named Balbir Singh Sodhi, who was gunned down in a Mesa, Arizona, gas station simply because he was dark-skinned and wore a turban.

On the same day as the Sodhi murder, September 15, 2001, Adel Karas, a forty-eight-year-old Egyptian Orthodox Coptic Christian and father of three, was viciously murdered outside his suburban Los Angeles import shop. That same day, a white supremacist in Texas went on a violent spree against brown-skinned men in retaliation for 9/11, murdering a Pakistani grocery store owner and a Hindu gas station owner and seriously wounding a Bangladeshi gas station operator. None of these victims' nations of origin, of course, had anything to do with the terror attacks against the World Trade Center and Pentagon. But logic rarely intrudes when it comes to hate crimes.

Ever since September 11, 2001, millions of Americans of Arab, Muslim, Sikh, and South Asian descent have been on their own version of orange alert, keenly aware that they can suddenly become the target of ignorant violence at the hands of their fellow Americans. And their places of worship—including Muslim mosques, Hindu temples and Sikh gurdwaras—have become inviting targets for patriotic terrorists seeking to lash out in blind rage at anyone who bears a resemblance to the foreign-looking people they've been programmed to hate.

After the massacre at the Oak Creek Sikh temple, I found myself frustatred—once again—by the double standard that the media applied to acts of terrorism, depending on the skin pigmentation and religious affiliation of the shooters and victims. "Well, I think that the one key thing that is missing from this entire debate is the [term] terrorism," I remarked on the Al-Jazeera English network shortly after the Oak Creek shooting. "Because that is exactly what it was. . . . If the white supremacy [and race-war views espoused by Wade

Michael Page, the gunman] are not political ideologies, then I don't know what is."

One of my copanelists on the Al-Jazeera English program that day was Professor Vijay Prashad, who holds the George and Martha Kellner Chair in South Asian History at Trinity College in Connecticut. Prashad observed that one of the most pernicious narratives coming out of the Oak Creek massacre was what he called the "wrong-address problem." This is the idea that the gunman's big mistake was picking the wrong target. "If Mr. Page had gone to a mosque [instead] . . . this would not be a mistake [in the eyes of many Americans]," according to Professor Prashad. "By saying that Sikhs are not Muslims, are people trying to say then that it's okay to go and kill Muslims or attack Muslim houses of worship? You know, the idea that [nearly] two billion Muslims are somehow responsible for whatever fantasy Mr. Page had put into his own head is extremely irresponsible."

In Page's mind, I later commented on the show, there was little difference between Sikhs and Muslims—they were all *foreign* and they were all threats to *his* America. "What Wade Page was doing was not just killing six people in a Sikh temple in Oak Creek, Wisconsin," I continued. "He was also sending a message to all brown people in America—to people in Muslim mosques, in Hindu temples, and Sikh temples around the country—that people like him are going to 'take back America.' . . . So this absolutely had a political ideology to it." It was, in short, terrorism—even if the US media gatekeepers refused to call it that.

Few people recall another act of terror, in November 2013, when one of America's busiest air terminals was gripped with panic as a gun-wielding terrorist walked around Los Angeles International Airport, firing his high-powered rifle. The shooter—a white, twenty-three-year-old, unemployed mechanic named Paul Anthony Ciancia—was on a deranged, anti-government mission that day to kill US Transportation Security Administration (TSA) guards. By the time Ciancia was finally shot and captured, he had killed one TSA guard and wounded two others, as well as a schoolteacher. Police found a note in the military fatigues he wore that day stating that he wanted "to kill TSA [agents] and pigs." Other writings by Ciancia referenced "New World Order" conspiracy theories—language, according to the Southern Poverty Law Center, that put him "squarely in the conspiracy-minded world of the antigovernment 'Patriot' movement." These so-called Patriots "increasingly see the DHS [Department of Homeland Security], which produces intelligence assessments of extremists that are distributed to other law enforcement agencies, as an enemy and even a collaborator in the New World Order conspiracy."

In the wake of yet another ideologically motivated, home-grown act of American terrorism, I again tried to point out the media's double standard when it came to covering mass shootings by white guys from the anti-government underground. The LAX shooting was being covered as simply another act of random violence, I said during an appearance on CNN with news anchor Carol Costello, despite the fact that the burst of violence had obvious political underpinnings. Ciancia, who had grown up in New Jersey, was seen as just one more guy who snapped. "These same right-wingers who always call for the 'racial profiling' of Arabs and Muslims after every terrorist attack will now be silent," I accurately predicted on CNN, "since they would now have to call for the racial profiling of every twentysomething white dude from New Jersey.... This would pretty much mean that the entire cast of [the MTV reality show] *Jersey Shore* should now be under NSA surveillance.

"All that I'm saying," I continued on CNN, "is that if it was a brown dude with an anti-government ideology, our entire American society would be calling it an act of terrorism.... And I think that Paul Anthony Ciancia should be called a terrorist."

Washington Post media reporter Paul Farhi investigated the double standard in coverage of terrorism in a June 2014 article titled "In the News Media, Are Muslims the Only 'Terrorists'?" In his article, Farhi examined the story of Jerad and Amanda Miller, a young married couple in Las Vegas who espoused an extremist anti-government ideology and went on a mass shooting spree in June 2014 (only one year before the San Bernardino attacks) which killed five people, including two uniformed police officers. Again, acting on their militant right-wing ideology, the Millers murdered two policemen, in addition to a third bystander, and then draped one of their victims in a Nazi banner and a "Don't Tread on Me" flag associated with anti-government movements.

Clearly a politically motivated act of terrorism, right? Not according to the press coverage of the crime.

"After [the Millers'] shooting spree . . . in Las Vegas, many in the media declined to use one potential label: terrorists," Farhi wrote in his *Washington Post* article. But there is no other way to describe the Millers. The couple expressed extreme anti-law enforcement and government views and supported the Patriot Movement. "We must . . . prepare for war," Jerad Miller once posted on Facebook. Stopping government "oppression," he wrote, "can only be accomplished by bloodshed." According to reports, the couple shouted out "Revolution!" after killing the police officers and entering a nearby Walmart store, where Amanda Miller shot a brave customer who tried to stop the gun-wielding couple before they killed themselves.

Syndicated cartoonist Darrin Bell brilliantly nailed the media double standard when it comes to covering terrorism in a drawing he did after Robert Dear's armed assault on the Colorado Planned Parenthood clinic. Bell's cartoon showed a copy of "The Equal Treatment Times" in a news rack. On the front page, next to the pop-eyed, looney-looking mug shot of Robert Dear familiar to all of us were these screaming headlines: PLANNED PARENTHOOD SHOOTER WAS "RADICALIZED" WHILE ATTENDING SERVICES AT FOX NEWS . . . DONALD TRUMP REFUSES TO RULE OUT FORCING ALL WHITE, CHRISTIAN PRO-LIFERS TO REGISTER IN DATA BASE.

Some vicious acts of "white terror" are directed specif ically at American Muslims, and *still* the American press can't bring itself to call this hate-inspired violence what it is. In February 2015, a forty-six-year-old gun-toting white man in North Carolina named Craig Stephen Hicks brutally executed three young Muslim college students in their own apartment at the University of North Carolina-Chapel Hill. Hicks systematically pumped bullets into the heads of the three students—Deah Shaddy Barakata, age twenty-three; Yusor Mohammad, twenty-one; and Razan Mohammad Abu Salha, nineteen—as if they were assassination targets.

Afterward, Hicks had the audacity to tell police that the cold-blooded executions he methodically carried out stemmed from a simple "parking dispute" in the apartment complex between him and the three innocent Muslim college students whom he executed in cold blood.

Give me a fucking break.

Dr. Mohammad Abu-Salha—the father of the two murdered young women, Yusor and Razan, and a psychiatrist by profession—had a more accurate assessment of the incident. Dr. Abu-Salha told the local newspaper that his daughters were killed in a hate crime. "This has all the signs. It was execution-style, a bullet in every head. This was not a dispute over a parking space. . . . This was a hate crime. . . . This man had picked on my daughter and her husband a couple of times before, and he talked with them with his gun in his belt. And they were uncomfortable with him, but they did not know he would go this far."

So, once again, let's review the facts. A man posts messages online glorying in the guns he owns and lashing out at the religions he hates, including Islam. "When it comes to insults, your religion [Islam] started this, not me," he once menacingly wrote. "If your religion [Islam] kept its big mouth shut, so would I." He then starts to harass and intimidate a young Muslim couple who are his neighbors. This campaign of abuse climaxes when he finally takes one of his beloved guns, enters his neighbors' apartment, and one by one executes the husband, wife, and her younger sister in cold blood, execution-style.

Now, I have spent my entire professional career as a Muslim public intellectual condemning terrorism in countless TV, radio, and print interviews, whenever these acts of mass murder are committed by those who share my Islamic faith. But it's also my job to denounce terrorism when it comes in other guises—even if others in the media refuse to accurately characterize these crimes, out of ignorance or prejudice. For example, in April 2014, I publicly stated that an attack on a Jewish community center near Kansas City, Missouri, by a white neo-Nazi gunman should have been framed as an act of "terrorism" within our media landscape. Similarly, if Craig Hicks had shot three Jewish students instead of young Muslims—after ranting about Judaism online- I would still adamantly be calling it an act of terrorism.

According to the FBI, the term "domestic terrorism" applies to any crime which:

- "Involves acts dangerous to human life that violate federal or state law;"
- "Appears intended to intimidate or coerce a civilian population; and"
- "Occur primarily within the territorial jurisdiction of the United States."

I can assure you that many of the some seven million Muslim Americans within the territorial jurisdiction of the United States felt intimidated by the cold-blooded executions carried out by Craig Hicks.

Tragically, terror violence against Muslim Americans is certain to grow as ruthless politicians and cynical media executives exploit the tensions generated by the endless wars in the Middle East, economic hardship, and cultural ignorance. Shortly after the Chapel Hill murders, I appeared on CNN again to discuss the growth of Islamophobia in the West today. When it comes to the portrayal of Muslims, I commented, if you look at the endless stream of sinister images and crude caricatures in TV news shows or Hollywood productions today, it's no wonder that those who embrace Islam are seen by many Americans as terrifying bogeymen.

The 2014 runaway hit movie *American Sniper,* with Bradley Cooper, glorified cutting down Iraqi Muslim men, women, and even children from a cold distance. Meanwhile TV shows like *Homeland,* with Claire Danes, while sometimes raising moral questions about the war on terror, nonetheless present CIA assassins with more humane compassion than the Muslims they target, who are inevitably portrayed as devilish figures operating, literally, in dark shadows.

Considering this constant media climate of suspicion and hostility, is it any wonder that the same week Craig Hicks was putting bullets in the heads of three innocent Muslim college students at UNC-Chapel Hill, a mosque was torched in Houston, Texas, and the Islamic School of Rhode Island in Providence had graffiti sprayed on the outside saying things like "Fuck Allah", "Muhammad is a Pedophile," and "Now THIS is a Hate Crime!"

After the Chapel Hill murders, I concluded my CNN interview on a grim note. "Islamophobia," I said, "is real and growing in America today."

Chapter Five

When Islamophobia Wears a Badge

T̲hough you might not know it from watching television, I can promise you that Muslims do not have a monopoly on terrorism. In fact, according to a 2015 report by the Southern Poverty Law Center, a domestic terrorist attack occurs (or is foiled) every thirty-four days in America. As the SPLC report concluded, "Muslim terrorists [only] accounted for a fraction of the total attacks" in America.

In the twelve years between 9/11 and 2013, more than three hundred Americans were killed on domestic soil by political violence or mass shootings—but only thirty-three of these fatalities were caused by extremists who were Muslim. Furthermore, according to the Southern Poverty Law Center report, the white supremacist terrorist Dylann Roof killed more human beings in one night alone in that historic South Carolina black church—nine defenseless people—than "Islamic terrorists have killed on US soil in total between 2011 and 2014."

In October 2014, I went on Don Lemon's prime-time CNN show—this was a few months before the *Do You Support ISIS?* interview heard around the world. On this occasion, I challenged Lemon's previous guest—former Republican presidential candidate Newt Gingrich, who has tried to hang onto the political spotlight by turning himself into a slayer of the Muslim bogeyman. I quoted CNN's own counterterrorism expert, Peter Bergen, who has written that "right-wing extremists in America have actually caused more damage and killed more Americans than jihadists have" in recent years. "You have more of a likelihood to die from drowning in your bathtub and getting struck by lightning than you do being killed by a jihadist," I told CNN viewers that day.

Despite the fact that white, right-wing extremists pose far more of a violent threat to Americans than jihadist radicals, US law enforcement authorities who monitor militant activity have turned American Muslims into their top target, simply on the basis of our religion. Long before 9/11, Muslims in the US were seen as a "model minority"—patriotic, hard-working, and family-oriented. But after years of media hysteria and political opportunism, Muslims are now seen as American pariahs, more reviled than any other group in our society. And law enforcement policies only reinforce this negative profiling. One of the worst offenders when it comes to anti-Muslim bias is the New York Police Department (NYPD).

Associated Press (AP) reporters Matt Apuzzo and Adam Goldman won the 2012 Pulitzer Prize for revealing that since 9/11, the NYPD had become one of "the country's most aggressive domestic intelligence agencies" and had consistently (and unconstitutionally) spied on the American Muslim community throughout the New York City metropolitan area for over a decade.

Using leaked internal NYPD documents, the AP reporters proved that the NYPD had used millions of taxpayer dollars to create an elaborate surveillance program that monitored and analyzed American Muslim daily life throughout New York City and surrounding states as well. The series of Pulitzer Prize–winning articles also revealed that the NYPD operated far outside of its own jurisdictional boundaries, targeting ethnic communities in ways that would run afoul of civil liberties laws if they were practiced by the federal government. Even more alarming, New York police officials did this with the "unprecedented help from the CIA in a partnership that has blurred the bright line between foreign and domestic spying."

Numerous media reports have also revealed that the NYPD has snooped on Muslim-neighborhood cafes and Islamic places of worship and even went so far as "infiltrating [college] student whitewater-rafting trips." New York police officials also sent undercover agents to spy on Muslim student groups in prestigious Ivy League colleges like the University of Pennsylvania and Yale University as well.

The NYPD spying program on Muslims, which was finally disbanded in April 2014 (at least officially), operated out of a department known internally as the "Demographics Unit." This bland, bureaucratic title masked an insidious program of ethnic and religious profiling. According to NYPD documents leaked to the press, the Demographics Unit spied on a variety of Muslim communities, including twenty-eight "ancestries of interest," receiving daily reports on life in New York-area Muslim neighborhoods from a network of paid informants and spies. The list of twenty-eight "ancestries of interest" put under daily surveillance by the NYPD included people who came from Muslim-majority countries in the Middle East and South Asia like Pakistan, Iran, Syria, and Egypt, as well as former Soviet states like Uzbekistan and Chechnya. The category "American Black Muslim" was also included on the NYPD watch list.

As part of its domestic spying proram, the NYPD sent undercover officers—known as "rakers"—into Muslim neighborhoods, where they focused on so-called hot spots, such as ethnic restaurants, Internet cafes, halal meat shops, and hookah bars. Capitalizing on its ability to recruit a diverse force of spies who spoke a variety of languages and dialects, the NYPD was able to infiltrate a wide spectrum of Muslim social life in the New York metropolitan area and beyond.

This sort of widespread, secret penetration of a community's daily life has sinister effects. "The NYPD's spying program has created psychological warfare in the [American Muslim] community," as Linda Sarsour, executive director of the Arab American Association of New York, told me during an interview in 2014. "The impact has been grave—with people suspecting fellow worshippers at mosques of being [NYPD] informants for simply trying to engage in political discussions. Whether you were a doctor, an imam, a teacher, a cab driver or a college student—no one was immune. Most startling of all has been the chilling effect on free speech and on the [political] organizing of Muslim student groups on many college campuses. Students are afraid that their activism will attract NYPD scrutiny."

"The NYPD has accepted and legitimized Islamophobia," Hofstra University adjunct professor Hussein Rashid told me in another interview on the subject. "Even with the disbanding of the so-called Demographics Unit, the culture created within the

NYPD, and projected onto New York City, will not disappear easily. It is a culture of fear, distrust, and implicit hatred of Muslims. It sits in the context of the broader racist practices that have become normalized in the NYPD, and is about making [American Muslims] feel powerless in front of them."

The CIA's close collaboration with the NYPD injected another ominous element into the domestic spying program. The CIA is forbidden by its founding charter from engaging in spy activity on American soil—a prohibition that the spy agency has often circumvented by working with metropolitan police departments like the NYPD. During the Cold War, New York police officials built their own CIA-connected espionage unit within their department—and this local-federal spy partnership continued into the War on Terror.

Exposure of the NYPD's Demographics Unit brought sharp rebukes from a number of political leaders in Washington. Among them was Senator Dianne Feinstein (D-Calif.), the chairwoman of the Senate Intelligence Committee, who stated that the CIA has "no business or authority in domestic spying or in advising the NYPD how to conduct local surveillance" against innocent members of the American Muslim community.

Congresswoman Judy Chu (D-Calif.) also expressed outrage about the collaboration between the CIA and NYPD. "I am shocked to hear that federal dollars may have helped finance the NYPD's misguided efforts to spy on Muslims in America," said Chu, one of thirty-four members of Congress who asked the Department of Justice and House Judiciary Committee to investigate the NYPD's Demographics Unit.

"In America, you don't put people under suspicion without good reason," said Congressman Rush Holt (D-NJ), who urged the Department of Justice to investigate the legality of the NYPD spying program. "The idea that people in a group [like Muslims] are suspect because of being members of a group is 'profiling', plain and simple."

Criticism of the NYPD program even came from within the FBI. "If you're sending an informant into a mosque when there is no evidence of wrongdoing, that's a very high-risk thing to do," said FBI General Counsel Valerie Caproni, referring to the New York Police Department's so-called mosque crawler program. "You're running right up against core constitutional rights. You're talking about freedom of religion." Ironically, the FBI uses similar profiling and monitoring techniques as the NYPD's Demographics Unit.

The NYPD would recruit its "mosque crawlers" by putting pressure on Muslims taken into custody for minor infractions, such as a traffic violation or a marijuana possession charge. If someone with a Muslim-sounding name or Middle Eastern ethnic background was placed under arrest, he or she would then be singled out for "extra" questioning. Those who agreed to cooperate with the NYPD spying program were promised leniency and even cash rewards.

For example, a nineteen-year-old American of Bangladeshi descent named Shamiur Rahman admitted that the NYPD paid him to go undercover and "bait" Muslims into saying inflammatory things. While leading his double life, Rahman took photos inside of mosques and collected names and information about innocent Muslims attending religious study groups.

"We need you to pretend to be one of them," Rahman recalled the NYPD telling him. "It's street theater," they once told him.

In a strategy called "create-and-capture," Rahman would strike up a conversation about jihad or terrorism with innocent people and then report back on the discussion to the NYPD. For his work, the young man was given as much as $1,000 a month and relief from his legal troubles after a string of minor marijuana arrests, which he was led to believe would lead to serious consequences if he did not become a police informant.

The NYPD spying program was a gross violation of religious freedom, infiltrating more than 250 mosques in New York and New Jersey. Even Islamic officials who fully cooperated with police authorities were not immune from surveillance.

For example, a New York imam named Reda Shata regularly worked with law enforcement officials, inviting police officers to his mosque for breakfast and even dining with then-Mayor Michael Bloomberg. But the NYPD was still spying on Shata the whole time, using two undercover agents to personally monitor the imam and at least two others to keep tabs on his mosque.

In the end, all this illegal snooping was for nothing. Despite its more than six years of spying on Muslim neighborhoods, mosques, and college activities, the NYPD's secretive Demographics Unit "never generated a [single] lead or triggered a terrorism investigation," according to departmental court testimony in August 2012.

But it took two more years and a concerted legal and political campaign to finally shut down the Big Brother surveillance program. In 2013, the American Civil Liberties Union, the CLEAR Project at City University of New York School of Law, and other plaintiffs filed a lawsuit, charging that the spy program violated "the Fourteenth Amendment's Equal Protection Clause and the First Amendment right to the free exercise of religion and guarantee of government neutrality toward religion." In addition, over 125 local and national organizations sent a jointly signed letter to the Department of Justice requesting that the federal government open an official civil rights investigation into the NYPD's warrantless Muslim surveillance program.

In September 2013, *The New York Times* editorial board strongly condemned the NYPD spying program on Muslims as completely "indefensible" and called for the establishment of "a police inspector general who can serve as a check against police abuses [of minority communities] in the future."

The NYPD's infiltration of Muslim student organizations and campus activities throughout the Northeast also elicited forceful condemnations. In October 2011, over forty professors at the City University of New York's Law School issued a public statement declaring that "the spying at CUNY campuses may have violated civil rights laws." Similarly, the Brooklyn College Faculty Council unanimously passed a resolution saying that the NYPD surveillance of student activities would also have a "chilling effect on the intellectual freedom necessary for a vibrant academic community."

"It's really about personal freedom," Moustafa Bayoumi, an English professor at Brooklyn College, said at the time. "The government, through the [NYPD], is working privately to destroy the private lives of Muslim citizens."

Finally, in April 2014, the NYPD officially announced that it would be ending the controversial Muslim spying program and closing the Demographics Unit which was primarily responsible for conducting surveillance on Muslim New Yorkers.

"Our administration has promised the people of New York a police force that keeps our city safe, but that is also respectful and fair," declared New York Mayor Bill de Blasio. "This reform is a critical step forward in easing tensions between the police and the [American Muslim] communities they serve, so that our cops and our citizens can help one another go after the real bad guys."

However, less than one month after the NYPD announced the end of its controversial spying program, *The New York Times* reported that the police department had not backed away from some of the program's more questionable initiatives—including pressuring Arab and Muslim men brought into police stations on minor charges to serve as informants. Among those the police continued to target as potential spies was a Muslim food-cart vendor, who was recruited after he came to a police station to dispute a parking ticket. In the first quarter of 2014 alone, the NYPD tried to recruit over 220 Muslims to spy on their communities.

While the NYPD's spying program generated intense controversy, it is far from the only agency that has indiscriminately invaded the privacy of law-abiding Muslim citizens. As Senator Richard Durbin (D-IL) has stated, "The FBI is [also] engaged in widespread surveillance of mosques and innocent American Muslims with no suspicion of wrongdoing." And considering the multitude of government security agencies—federal, state, and local—as well as private security contractors that have proliferated since 9/11, the NYPD and FBI are just the tip of the surveillance iceberg.

It is a dangerous and slippery slope when society singles out one group for special security treatment, based only on their religion, race or ethnicity. In the frenzy following 9/11, many innocent American Muslims were rounded up and subjected to physical abuse and indefinite, unwarranted confinement. Now, following Paris and San Bernardino, we hear serious political proposals for registering, banning, and imprisoning Muslims in detention centers, as Japanese Americans were during World War II, to our country's lasting shame.

This is the way a civilized society begins to devour itself. By allowing our political leaders and law enforcement officials to scapegoat one segment of our population—to turn innocent people into targets of suspicion, into the *enemy*—we demean all that is good and decent about our nation.

The public outcry over the surveillance of American Muslims culminated in June 2013 when the ACLU, NYCLU, and the CLEAR Project at CUNY Law School filed a lawsuit against the NYPD's "discriminatory and unjustified surveillance of New York Muslims." It wasn't until January 2016 that the lawsuit was finally settled and the NYPD was barred from carrying out investigations on the basis of race, religion, or ethnicity. Furthermore, the settlement discredited the NYPD's 2007 "Radicalization in the West" report and ordered it to be removed from their website.

CHAPTER 6

What Would Muhammad Do?

In September 2005, almost a decade before the world outside Paris became shockingly aware of the French satirical magazine *Charlie Hebdo*, there was a small newspaper in Denmark called *Jyllands-Posten* which published a series of twelve cartoon caricatures of Islam's beloved Prophet Muhammad (peace be upon him, or pbuh). These silly cartoons in an obscure Danish newspaper would be the first major geopolitical flashpoint in the current culture war revolving around Islam.

According to BBC World News, one of the most controversial cartoon images published by *Jyllands-Posten* at the time depicted the Prophet carrying a lit bomb in the shape of a turban on his head decorated with the Shahada (the Islamic declaration of faith). The cartoons depicted the Prophet Muhammad (pbuh) as "angry, dangerous-looking—a stereotypical villain with heavy, dark eyebrows and whiskers," according to BBC News.

In response to this sacrilegious assault on Islam's most revered figure, on October 19, 2005, several prominent ambassadors from over ten Muslim countries requested a meeting with Anders Fogh Rasmussen, the Danish prime minister at the time, to discuss the inflammatory cartoons.

He refused to meet with them.

Shortly after, global protests and violent riots over the Danish cartoons began to erupt around the Muslim world. In the wake of this upheaval, I joined a small delegation of American Muslim leaders at a meeting at the Norwegian Embassy in Washington, D.C. During our meeting with the Norwegian ambassador to the United States—who attempted to fill the political vacuum left by Danish authorities—he emphasized to us that *Jyllands-Posten* was nothing more than a right-wing newspaper with a limited circulation and it was undoubtedly trying to provoke controversy to pump up sales.

The ambassador's diplomatic message reinforced the only rational conclusion that any reasonable person could make: it was clear that the publication of these inflammatory cartoons was purposefully done to incite violence by Muslims. Unfortunately for the whole world, some thuggish and idiotic Muslims took the newspaper's bait without blinking. Shortly after the publication of the cartoons, several Danish and Norwegian embassies in Beirut and Damascus were attacked by angry protestors. In Lebanon, some of these protests soon escalated into physical violence between Muslims and Christians, and some demonstrators even bizarrely threw rocks at a Maronite Catholic church, bringing back memories of the civil war that once gripped the Lebanese capital. Meanwhile, the global firestorm over the cartoons raged across the Internet, with one militant website calling for an "embassy-burning day."

Though it should go without saying, these days it's necessary to remind people that the vast majority of the some 1.7 billion Muslims across the world simply ignored the cartoon tempest. As a global Muslim community, it is our primary religious and moral obligation to reflect on our own internal shortcomings and collectively clean our "own house" (through nonviolent means) before we can ever rightfully expect any sort of sympathy for our political grievances in the global marketplace of ideas.

Meanwhile, the Western press was doing its own soul-searching on the Danish cartoon controversy. Most journalists in the West (including myself) acknowledged that these silly cartoons had every legal right to be published. But just because something has the *legal* right to be published does not automatically mean that it should be deemed *worthy* of publication. By publishing the scurrilous and sophomoric cartoons under the false banner of "free speech," the *Jyllands-Posten* editors knew what they were really doing was stirring up more fury and hatred in a powder-keg world where many Muslims already felt under assault from the West. The Danish newspaper editors did this for entirely cynical reasons, as the Norwegian diplomat observed—it was nothing more than a circulation stunt, and a wildly reckless one at that.

To their credit, many prominent Western journalists, reporters and editors around the world immediately saw through the *Jyllands-Posten*'s disingenuous free press argument. *The Washington Post*'s executive editor, Leonard Downie Jr., decided against reprinting the cartoons, explaining, "This newspaper vigorously exercises its freedom of expression every day. In doing so, we have standards for accuracy, fairness and taste that our readers have come to expect from *The Post*. We decided that publishing these cartoons would violate our [editorial] standards." Echoing Downie's decision, *The Washington Post*'s editorial page editor, Fred Hiatt, stated: "I would not have chosen to publish them, given that they were designed to provoke and did not, in my opinion, add much to any important debate."

The blatant hypocrisy of the *Jyllands-Posten*'s free speech argument was made clear a few weeks after the furor over the Danish cartoons began to die down, when *The Guardian* revealed, "The Danish newspaper that first published the cartoons of the prophet Muhammad that have caused a storm of protest throughout the Islamic world refused to run drawings lampooning Jesus Christ." According to *The Guardian*, a Danish cartoonist named Christoffer Zieler submitted a series of sacrilegious cartoons dealing with the resurrection of Jesus Christ to *Jyllands-Posten* for publication. But Zeiler received a rejection letter from one of the newspaper's editors, who told the cartoonist:

> I don't think *Jyllands-Posten*'s readers will enjoy the [Jesus] drawings. As a matter of fact, I think that they will provoke an outcry. . . .Therefore, I will not use them. . . .

In other words, *Jyllands-Posten* was all for free speech when it came to demeaning the holiest figure in Islam, but not the holiest figure in Christianity.

There is no respectable publication in the Western world that would run racist or anti-Semitic cartoons, nor should they. Likewise, I applaud the decision made by Western newspapers like *The Washington Post* against running the hateful Danish cartoons. And, by the way, I condemn any newspaper in the Arab and Muslim world that publishes anti-Semitic cartoons or articles. To these newspaper editors, I would simply ask how they can claim to have any moral authority to be upset about anti-Muslim cartoons in the Western press when they shamefully carry the same sort of anti-Semitic hate cartoons on a regular basis in their own pages. This underlines the need for the global Muslim community to put our own house in order as well. As our religion teaches, we have a collective moral responsibility to make certain that every type of racism, xenophobia, and religious bigotry is eradicated from our respective communities.

In 2010, a new round of cartoon madness broke out, this time in the United States, when Trey Parker and Matt Stone, the creators of *South Park*, chose to depict the Prophet Muhammad (pbuh) disguised in a bear costume for the two hundredth episode of the popular cartoon show. What many people did not realize was that Parker and Stone had already portrayed him on *South Park* over nine years earlier, in a July 2001 episode called "Super Best Friends"—without provoking any controversy whatsoever. During that earlier episode, there was a funny scene in which "Super Best Friends" Jesus, Buddha, and Muhammad (peace be upon all of them) were depicted as righteous crime-fighting superheroes. The key difference, of course, is that this earlier episode was aired two months *before* 9/11.

I guess those were more peaceful and forgiving times.

By the time the 2010 *South Park* episode was broadcast, zealotry was in the air, across the religious spectrum, and two extremist buffoons with a no name website called Revolution Muslim posted a thinly veiled threat against the show's creators. Following the famous journalism adage "If it bleeds, it leads," we saw much of the mainstream media immediately giving a global platform to these unknown knuckleheads, which only helped to tarnish the reputation of Muslims in America even further.

Once again, it was far sexier for the media to report the inflammatory message of two no-name idiots with a website rather than tell the stories of the many unheralded Muslims in business, medicine, education, sports, and entertainment who were making the world a better place. The vast percentage of Muslims, of course, simply went about their lives, too busy to get caught up in yet another media-manufactured frenzy over the depiction of Islam's prophet. As I stated in my CNN column on the *South Park* controversy: "In any free democratic society, the concept of free speech can only be combated with more free speech, not censorship. If the creators of *South Park* choose to depict the Prophet Muhammad, that is their First Amendment right, and they should be able to do so freely without any threats of physical violence and retribution."

Unfortunately, after the silly *South Park* controversy, things only got weirder in cartoon land. A Seattle cartoonist named Molly Norris decided to declare May 20, 2010, to be "Draw Muhammad Day" in order to promote free speech among her fellow cartoonists. In doing so, Norris innocently "created a poster-like cartoon showing many objects—from a cup of coffee to a box of pasta to a tomato—all claiming to be the likeness of Muhammad," according to an article in *The Los Angeles Times*.

Norris told a Seattle radio talk show host that she came up with the idea for "Draw Muhammad Day" because "as a cartoonist, I just felt so much passion about what had happened [with the *South Park* controversy]," noting that "it's a cartoonist's job to be non-PC [politically correct]." However, she quickly backtracked once her Muhammad cartoon poster began to go viral on the Internet, where all hell predictably broke loose. When she later disavowed her "Draw Muhammad Day" campaign, *The Los Angeles Times* asked her why she had launched it in the first place. "Because I'm an idiot," Miss Norris replied. "This particular cartoon of a 'poster' seems to have struck a gigantic nerve, something I was totally unprepared for."

Tragically, nearly six years later, Molly Norris is apparently still in hiding because of death threats that she received. A January 2015 CNN article noted that Norris' name even popped up on Al-Qaeda's most-wanted list in a jihadist magazine called *Inspire*. The article also noted that this hit list also included *Charlie Hebdo* editor Stéphane Charbonnier, who was murdered along with nine others that same month in the attacks on the magazine office in Paris.

"I didn't mean for my satirical poster to be taken seriously. It became kind of an excuse for people to hate or be mean-spirited. I'm not mean-spirited," Norris told *City Arts Magazine* in response to her unwanted notoriety.

In an effort to calm the madness, Norris made a short film about the experiences of American Muslim women who wear hijab (or headscarves) to try countering anti-Muslim stereotypes. "[But] it was too late and the death threats too many," wrote CNN journalist Steve Almasy about Norris, who changed her identity and remains in hiding.

Meanwhile, in another example of crazy overreaction stemming from the *South Park* controversy, the two young American Muslim converts who made the vaguely threatening remarks on their obscure website were arrested and sentenced to harsh prison sentences for their inflammatory language, with one receiving twenty-five years in federal prison and the other eleven and a half years. While not excusing their idiotic threatening remarks, there is clearly once again a double standard at work in a society where authorities look the other way when fundamentalist Christians and right-wing extremists make similarly threatening statements about women's health providers, as well as Muslim, Jewish, and African American leaders and others they regard as their mortal enemies.

Let's pause at this point for a message on behalf of sanity.

I address this message to my fellow Muslims around the world. Please understand that the First Amendment of the United States Constitution allows for the broad exercise of free speech, even for language that can be deemed racist, xenophobic, anti-Semitic, Islamophobic, or homophobic. We know that there will always be people who, for their own hateful reasons, will fully exploit the constitutional right of free speech to denigrate minorities. This is an inevitable part of life in a free society. So ask yourselves, my fellow Muslims, how would our beloved Prophet Muhammad (peace be upon him) respond to such silly provocations as the Danish and *South Park* and *Charlie Hebdo* cartoons if he were alive today?

He would do absolutely nothing.

All of my fellow Muslims should be aware of a well-known Islamic parable about how the Prophet reacted to hostile insults directed toward him. As the story goes, the Prophet Muhammad (pbuh) would regularly walk by the house of an unruly female neighbor, who used to curse him violently and would then proceed to dump garbage onto him from her window every time he would walk by her house. One day, the Prophet noticed that the woman was not present to dump garbage onto him as he passed under her window. In an act of true prophetic kindness, he went out of his way to inquire about her well-being and when he found out that she had fallen ill, he paid visits to this unfriendly neighbor at her sickbed. This kindness toward overtly hostile neighbors is the "Ubuntu" standard to which every Muslim should aspire—instead of responding with violent threats whenever we are insulted or provoked.

So any time we see a bunch of silly cartoons waved in our faces, every Muslim around the world should take a deep breath and simply ask ourselves one basic question:

"What would Prophet Muhammad do?"

And then repeat after me: absolutely nothing.

Of course, not all of those who seek to ridicule and demean Islam are sophomoric cartoonists. There are also a number of political and religious figures in the West who have built entire careers on offending Muslims. One such professional provocateur is the notorious right-wing Dutch politician Geert Wilders, who made international headlines in 2008 when he released a fifteen-minute online video titled *Fitna* (Arabic for "strife"), aimed at stoking anti-Muslim fear around the world. The film opens with a controversial caricature of the Prophet Muhammad—one of the twelve cartoons that ignited the Danish controversy—followed by predictably provocative, cherry-picked verses from the Quran juxtaposed with graphic images of the September 11, 2001, terror attacks and harrowing audio clips from 911 calls made by victims trapped inside the World Trade Center. Wilders' propaganda video also includes a series of newspaper headlines suggesting that European democracy is under threat from Islamic beliefs and practices, and that some Muslims want to create Islamic states in Europe. Muslim spokespersons in the West, including yours truly, condemned the Wilders video as an obvious attempt to fan the flames of Islamophobia, and in a March 2008 CNN article I predicted that Muslims would not take the bait this time. "We in the global community learned a lot from the Danish cartoon controversy," I commented at the time. "I don't think it will be anything remotely like that."

This time, even the prime minister of Holland, Jan Peter Balkenende, condemned the Islamophobic video as a blatant attempt to incite hatred and bloodshed. "The film equates Islam with violence. . . . We [the Dutch government] reject this interpretation," stated Balkenende. "The vast majority of Muslims reject extremism and violence. . . . In fact, the victims [of terrorism] are often also Muslims."

But as we all know, there is good money to be made in the Islamophobia business today. According to a

September 2012 Reuters article, Wilders received sub-stantial funding from anti-Islam groups in America after his controversial video was released. Some of the money raised in the United States went to cover legal expenses for Wilders, who was facing growing litigation in Holland for his hate film. Among those in America who inevitably rushed to support Wilders was Pamela Geller, though she herself stopped short of giving him money.

Meanwhile, back in America, money-chasing preachers and Muslim-baiters were also seeking to cash in on the Islamophobia boom. Prominent among these hate hucksters was Terry Jones, the Quran-burning pastor from Florida who, with his handlebar mustache and wraparound shades, looks more like a *Sons of Anarchy* biker than a man of the cloth. Jones, author of a book unambiguously titled *Islam Is the Devil*, proceeded to stir up so much fury around the world—with the help of the 24/7 media circus—that President Obama and General David Petraeus, commander of Western forces in Afghanistan at the time, felt compelled to call on him to cease and desist, pointing out that his Quran-burning stunt was increasing the risk to American soldiers overseas.

"Look, this is a recruitment bonanza for [groups like ISIS and] Al-Qaeda," President Obama told ABC's *Good Morning America*. "You know, you could have serious violence in places like Pakistan and Afghanistan. This could increase the recruitment of individuals who would be willing to blow themselves up in American cities or European cities."

Despite widespread condemnation from political and military leaders, Jones' publicity stunt produced copycat Quran-burning campaigns at mosques in other states, including Tennessee and Michigan, where other media-whoring preachers could always count on attracting camera crews.

At the time, I predicted on CNN that we had not seen the last of the Quran-burning craze, since the media seemed so eager to fan these flames. And, in fact, the controversy burst into flame again a few years later in Afghanistan when American soldiers stupidly tried to burn about five hundred copies of the Quran, as part of what *The Washington Post* described as a "badly bungled" security sweep at an Afghan prison. The US soldiers went ahead with their bonfire despite repeated warnings from Afghan soldiers that they were making a colossal cultural mistake. The Quran burnings triggered massive protests across Afghanistan and, according to some analysts, might have also played a role in the increased attacks against NATO troops by Afghan soldiers and police shortly thereafter.

As I told National Public Radio (NPR) host Michel Martin in February 2012, in our tinderbox world, highly provocative acts like the incineration of Muslim holy books can be expected to ignite violent reactions—and in fact that's what provocateurs like Terry Jones aim to do, to light their names in the sky at the expense of others' safety and lives.

Media stunts like Jones's have real-world consequences. They reinforce deeply held suspicions in the Muslim world that the West has no respect for its beliefs and practices. As I told NPR during that interview, these suspicions are reinforced when Muslims see other outrageous images like the "video of American soldiers urinating on Afghani corpses . . . [a] violation of the Geneva Conventions, which is something that even the Pentagon has admitted. . . . You would figure after a decade in Afghanistan, we would be a little more culturally aware of a country that we've been occupying and it's clear that we've not reached that point yet."

Before the infamous January 2015 terrorist attacks that became worldwide headlines, most people are unaware that the French satirical magazine *Charlie Hebdo* had long been the source of controversy for its anti-Muslim cartoons in the past. In November 2011, the *Charlie Hebdo* offices were badly damaged by a firebomb after it had published a spoof issue that was "guest edited" by the Prophet Muhammad to commemorate the electoral victory of an Islamist party in the former French colony of Tunisia. Media reports also stated that hackers had disrupted the magazine's website on that same day.

Despite the magazine's blatant disrespect for their religion, it is important to note that French Muslim leaders strongly condemned the 2011 attack on *Charlie Hebdo* immediately after the attack. Mohammed Moussaoui, head of the French Council of the Muslim Faith, declared that his group "reaffirms with force its total opposition to all acts and all forms of violence" against the magazine. "I think that [the attackers] are themselves unbelievers. . . . Idiots who betray their own religion."

I could not have said it better myself, monsieur.

Unfortunately, the world has only continued to spin more out of control since the 2011 assault on *Charlie Hebdo*, with the most extreme and militant forces on all sides holding the world hostage to their idiocy.

On January 7, 2015, a small black Citroen car with two masked gunmen, dressed in black and armed with Kalashnikov assault rifles, approached the *Charlie Hebdo* offices at 10 Rue Nicolas-Appert in Paris. The two gunmen were brothers named Cherif and Said Kouachi. For the following three days, they would create a reign of terror in the French capital and inspire an entire new wave of Islamophobia around the world with their acts of wanton violence that would certainly make the Prophet Muhammad shed tears of sadness if he were alive today.

Once inside the *Charlie Hebdo* building, the two brothers began opening fire, killing ten people in the magazine office. Witnesses said they had heard the gunmen shouting, "We have avenged the Prophet Muhammad" and "God is Great" in Arabic while going about their unholy business. Later, the marauding brothers shot down two policemen as they fled the scene, including a French Muslim officer named Ahmed Merabet who was murdered in cold blood as he lay wounded on the sidewalk. "He was killed by false Muslims," the police officer's brother defiantly told reporters.

The brothers' mad murder spree continued over the following two days, as a French policewoman was shot down and an accomplice of the Kouachis killed four innocent people at a kosher grocery store. The Kouachi brothers finally holed themselves up in a printing factory on the outskirts of Paris, which was soon surrounded by hundreds of armed officers. Telling the media they wanted to die as "martyrs," they achieved their goal by running from the building with guns blazing.

After this spasm of Paris violence, I was once again drafted by the media to be "the Muslim Guy," forced to defend the millions of my fellow peaceful coreligionists. On that first night of the *Charlie Hebdo* attacks alone, I had three major primetime television interviews on MSNBC, Al-Jazeera English, and finally my soon-to-be notorious interview on CNN with Don "Do You Support ISIS?" Lemon.

On the MSNBC show *All In with Chris Hayes*, I repeated my long-held conviction that people of all backgrounds should stand together "against any sort of violence perpetrated against people who are just trying to exercise free speech." At the same time, I also tried to educate viewers about the growing vilification of Muslims in the Western media and the double standard that allows such blatant bigotry. I observed that "no Western liberal newspaper on the face of the earth would publish anti-Semitic cartoons—and rightfully so—for understandable reasons." But *Charlie Hebdo*'s mean-spirited cartoons against the Muslim faith simply brought shrugs, or chuckles, from France's culturally savvy liberal champagne class.

I also reminded MSNBC host Chris Hayes that one of the seventeen victims of the *Charlie Hebdo* attacks was a brave Muslim police officer who had tried to stop the attackers. Finally, I said on MSNBC that night, despite whatever the Kouachi brothers were screaming as they fired their guns, their crimes were in no way justified by the teachings of Islam. "The Prophet Mohammed was insulted many times during his life and never once did he order to kill anybody in retribution," I said. "This is pure mass murder, plain and simple . . . a crime against humanity."

My blunt condemnation of the Kouachis' vile deeds was echoed by other prominent Muslims, including my dear friend Reza Aslan, who joined me on NBC's *Meet the Press* that Sunday in the midst of the *Charlie Hebdo* frenzy. Aslan strongly rejected the noxious assertion that mainstream Muslims were largely silent about acts of terrorism like the Paris attacks. "Let's be clear that every single Muslim organization and prominent individual, be it political or religious leaders, everyone has condemned [the *Charlie Hebdo* attacks and] every attack that occurs in the name of Islam," Aslan firmly stated. "Anyone who keeps saying that we need to hear the moderate voices of Islam, why aren't Muslim denouncing these violent attacks, doesn't [know how to use] Google."

To illustrate this point even further, if you Google the words "Muslim condemn terrorism" (without quotes), you will receive over 15,500,000 results.

But there is a difference between denouncing the ugly violence that took the lives of seventeen innocent people in Paris in January 2015 and celebrating the so-called editorial boldness of *Charlie Hebdo*. As I have publicly stated many times, I strongly support the right of free speech—in fact, I'm constantly under attack for exercising that right as a Muslim public intellectual. Nevertheless, I see nothing honorable about a magazine that pumps up its circulation by again and again heaping mockery and scorn on people who inhabit the substrata of France, men and women who already suffer the stings of prejudice every day. As I remarked earlier, civilized society in the West allows a kind of vicious bigotry when it comes to Muslims that it would never permit with other minorities.

Adding insult to the humiliation that French Muslims feel at the hands of *Charlie Hebdo* cartoonists, four months after the January 2015 attacks, the literary organization PEN American Center decided to honor the French magazine with its 2015 PEN/Toni and James C. Goodale Freedom of Expression Courage Award. To their credit, over two hundred prominent PEN authors—including Junot Diaz, Joyce Carol Oates, and Michael Ondaatje—publicly objected to the 2015 PEN award in a passionately worded open letter, which included the following:

> It is clear and inarguable that the murder of a dozen people in the *Charlie Hebdo* offices is sickening and tragic. What is neither clear nor inarguable is the decision to confer an award for courageous freedom of expression on *Charlie Hebdo*, or what criteria, exactly were used to make that decision. . . .
>
> Power and prestige are elements that must be recognized in considering almost any form

of discourse, including satire. The inequities between the person holding the pen and the subject fixed on paper by that pen cannot, and must not, be ignored. . . .

To the section of the French population that is already marginalized, embattled, and victimized, a population that is shaped by the legacy of France's various colonial enterprises, and that contains a large percentage of devout Muslims, *Charlie Hebdo's* cartoons of the Prophet must be seen as being intended to cause further humiliation and suffering. . . .

Our concern is that, by bestowing the Toni and James C. Goodale Freedom of Expression Courage Award on *Charlie Hebdo*, PEN is not simply conveying support for freedom of expression, but also valorizing selectively offensive material: material that intensifies the anti-Islamic, anti-Maghreb, anti-Arab sentiments already prevalent in the Western world. . . . "

As if to prove that the January 2015 massacre would have no effect on its editorial independence—or its sense of wisdom and compassion—*Charlie Hebdo* has continued to take every opportunity to offend Muslims, even the weakest and most suffering. In September 2015, the magazine took aim at, of all targets, the three-year-old Syrian refugee named Aylan Kurdi, whose death shocked the conscience of millions worldwide when the harrowing image of his small corpse washed up on the shores of the Mediterranean was caught by a photographer.

In a display of depraved editorial judgment, *Charlie Hebdo* ran a cartoon image of the now-iconic dead child, accompanied by a series of captions, each more sick and less funny than the next.

"Welcome to migrants!"

"So near his goal!"

"Promo! 2 kids menus for the price of one." (This one was featured on a sign carried by a Ronald McDonald clown as he strolled along the beach.) Another cartoon in the magazine depicted Jesus standing next to the drowned infant, with this caption: "Proof that Europe is Christian. Christians walk on water—Muslim children sink."

Peter Herbert, chair of the British Society of Black Lawyers and former vice chair of the Metropolitan Police Authority in London, spoke for many around the world when he denounced *Charlie Hebdo*'s decision to run the dead baby cartoons. The magazine, Herbert declared, is a "racist, xenophobic and ideologically bankrupt publication that represents the moral decay of France." He added, "The Society of Black Lawyers will consider reporting this as [an] incitement to hate crime and persecution before the International Criminal Court."

It is difficult to simply turn one's cheek when one is struck in the face, whether literally or figuratively, as Christians—and Muslims and Jews—down through the ages have learned, despite their religious teachings. But that is what we must do, unless we want the world to descend any further into brutality and misery.

"Muslims should ignore these provocations," said Zaytuna College cofounder Imam Zaid Shakir. He cited *The Innocence of Muslims*, the anti-Islam film released online in 2012, which some people believed might have been a cause for the storming of the US consulate in Benghazi, Libya, which took the lives of US Ambassador Christopher Stevens and three others. If the crudely made film had simply been ignored by the global Muslim community, Shakir observed, it would have "died a natural death with less than 50 views on YouTube." Instead, the film sparked a global storm in the Muslim world, and ended up with over fifteen million views on YouTube within a very short period of time. "As a community," Shakir told me, "we have to learn the keep the tempest in a teapot" and ignore the stupid and vicious insults coming our way.

But when the provocation becomes so persistent and so obscene that it simply can't be ignored, what then? Peter Herbert has suggested the proper response, in the case of *Charlie Hebdo*'s latest assault on human decency. Public shaming and protest is in order, and then perhaps legal action. But violence is never the solution. It only sends the world spiraling further down to a dark and dangerous place. Shedding innocent blood is a violation of all that is holy within us, no matter what religion we embrace.

CHAPTER 7

We Are All Scapegoats

I once gave a speech at Harvard University entitled "Media Madness and Minority Stereotypes" on Islamophobia and the future of Muslims in the Western world. During my Harvard talk, I highlighted that the rise of Islamophobia today is only the most recent chapter of Western "demonization" of minority groups based on race, religion and ethnicity. Ever since 9/11, Muslim Americans and Arab Americans—once regarded as solid citizens, with a strong commitment to family, faith, and country—have become the leading scapegoats in America today. We have now joined a long esteemed line of demonized minorities—from American Indians to Asian immigrants to African Americans to the LGBT community. After Paris and San Bernardino, the pitchfork and torch brigades are braying for Muslim blood more loudly than ever, with Donald Trump leading the way.

The irony, of course, is that not long ago, it was Trump's own ancestors—German American immigrants—who were the demons of the day, as the United States fought two world wars against Germany. The only thing that saved Trump's people from being rounded up and put in camps during World War II, like Japanese American families—as Trump lauded President Franklin Roosevelt for doing—was that their skin color happened to be white. Those who are so eager to stigmatize Muslims today should keep this in mind—next time around it could be them. That's the way these American nativist, "know-nothing" uprisings work. One day it's Catholics who are the reviled aliens, then it's Jewish people, then it's Muslims. If you don't belong to one of these groups, just wait your turn—you could be next in line.

We will always be subjected to these us-versus-them hysteria campaigns as long as people in power seek to divide Americans for their own cynical political purposes—whether it's to whip up war fever, split apart working people, or simply keep the citizenry fearful and easier to manipulate.

It was during World War I when the US government, under President Woodrow Wilson, began to perfect the techniques of mass propaganda and fear-mongering. Knowing that the disastrous European war he was intent on joining was unpopular at home, President Wilson created the Committee on Public Information—better known as the "Creel Committee," after its chairman, the pro-war journalist George Creel—which subjected Americans to a nationwide blitz of pro-war brainwashing. The Creel Committee's advertising campaigns depicted the German enemy as the "brutal Hun"— "bloodthirsty savages" who were guilty of the most heinous and depraved acts. This demonization of the German foe inevitably infected public perceptions of German Americans at home.

In 1917, when the United States entered the war in Europe, there were about eight million people of German heritage living in the United States, nearly 10 percent of the entire population, making them the largest minority group in the country. Despite their prominence in American life and their sturdy reputation as an industrious, well-educated, law-abiding group, German Americans soon found themselves the target of a variety of persecutions and humiliations, from the serious to the petty. Authorities warned citizens to keep a close eye on their German neighbors and report any suspicious activity. German-language newspapers were shut down, German American religious services were disrupted, and the churches were painted yellow. As American soldiers began dying in the war, the hysteria grew worse and German Americans were subjected to mob violence. People of German descent were dragged from their homes at night and forced to kiss the American flag or sing "The Star-Spangled Banner." In one of the most notorious examples of vigilante action, a German immigrant in Illinois who was accused by his neighbors of stealing dynamite was dragged out of town, stripped, and lynched.

The Creel Committee's jingoistic propaganda efforts only made life worse for the millions of innocent German Americans. The committee encouraged the elimination of German-language instruction in public schools and even urged renaming sauerkraut "liberty cabbage" and German measles "liberty measles"—a flight of absurdity echoed years later by moronic Republican congressional leaders, who demanded that "french fries" be called "freedom fries" in response to France's wise opposition to the US invasion of Iraq.

For the safety of their community, many German Americans began Americanizing the spelling of their last names, changing "Schmidt," for example, to "Smith." And cities with large German populations leaned over backward to prove their patriotism, with Cincinnati passing a law that removed German pretzels from lunch counters, and Pittsburgh even banning the public performance of music by Beethoven.

During World War II, of course, it was Japanese Americans' turn to become scapegoats. Like the German-Americans before them, Japanese Americans were known as hard-working, family-oriented citizens, who had built a stake in the American dream by becoming farmers and opening small businesses. But the path to their wartime stigmatizing was paved by decades of "yellow peril" hate-mongering along the West Coast, particularly in California. Under the Immigration Act of 1924, Asians were even prohibited from attaining US citizenship. Considering this history of racial profiling, it should come as little surprise that many Americans reacted with hatred and anger when the Japanese military attacked the United States Navy at Pearl Harbor on December 7, 1941. Japan's military victories in the Pacific only intensified the anti-Japanese feelings in the United States.

Similar to the rounding up of American Muslim, Arab, and South Asian males after the 9/11 attacks, within forty-eight hours of the air assault on Pearl Harbor, over 1,200 Japanese American men were arrested. Most would be incarcerated for the entire four-year duration of the Second World War. They would soon be joined by thousands more men, women, and children of Japanese descent.

Even hard-nosed FBI Director J. Edgar Hoover conceded that the decision to detain Japanese Americans in internment camps was "based primarily on public and political pressures rather than factual data" about domestic security. In making his fateful decision about Japanese Americans, President Franklin Roosevelt relied heavily on the analysis of General John Dewitt, chief of the Western Defense Command, whose flagrant racism was immortalized in quotes such as "Once a Jap, always a Jap" and "The Japanese race is an enemy race."

Based on General Dewitt's horribly racist recommendations, by June 1942, more than 110,000 people of Japanese descent (more than 70 percent of whom were American citizens) had been forced from their homes and transported to ten different internment camps scattered throughout the inhospitable desert regions of the American West. Most of these innocent Japanese Americans would be forced to live in these remote, desolate camps throughout the entire war—as strangers in their own land.

It is very instructive to recall this shameful period in American history during these current times, when madness once again fills the air, along with talk of mass registration, detention, or even banning of Muslims. Ominously, the detention of Japanese Americans during the 1940s was accompanied by the same political hate language and media smears that we hear today against Muslims. Just as American TV and film productions today are stuffed with Muslim villains, hideous caricatures

of Japanese were featured in Hollywood movies, maga-
zines, and newspapers during World War II.

Most people know Theodore "Dr. Seuss" Geisel as
one of the most beloved and best-selling American chil
dren's authors of all time. But few know that during his
early years as an aspiring editorial cartoonist, Geisel
drew some of the most viciously demeaning images of
Japanese for American newspapers and war bonds campaigns. "Slap That Jap—Bug Swatters Cost Money," went
one of Geisel's war bond posters, showing a bespecta-
cled, buck-toothed Emperor Hirohito as a grotesque fly-
ing insect.

Of course, no group in our country has had to
endure more systematic abuse and degradation historically than African Americans in United States history.
As with Japanese during World War II and Muslim
Americans during the War on Terror, the racist policies directed at blacks were reinforced by centuries of
white supremacy and cultural stereotyping. One of the
first silent films in history, D.W. Griffith's *The Birth of a
Nation*, released in 1915, set the tone with its depiction
of black men as stupid, brutal, lust-driven beasts (gro-
tesquely played by white actors in black face), whom
only the heroic gallantry of the Ku Klux Klan could
keep in check.

The Birth of a Nation unleashed a flood of racial
demons in America, with no less than President

Woodrow Wilson—like Griffith, a fellow Southern white supremacist—hailing the "terrible" truth of the movie. ("It is like writing history in lightning," enthused President Wilson at the time.) The film led to a revival of the Ku Klux Klan and inspired a new wave of lynchings in the South.

It's taken many years for our country to understand the full, sinister impact of race lynchings on the American psyche. Even today, scholars debate the actual number of black men, women, and children who fell victim to this savage method of racial repression. According to widely covered 2105 report by the Equal Justice Institute, nearly four thousand black people were killed in "racial terror lynchings" in a dozen Southern states between 1877 and 1950. "Lynchings were violent and public acts of torture that traumatized black people throughout the country and were largely tolerated by state and federal officials," the report noted. "These lynchings were terrorism."

In the wake of this eye-opening report, *The New York Times* editorialized, "It is important to remember that the hangings, burnings and dismemberments of black American men, women and children that were relatively common in this country between the Civil War and World War II were often public events." These "events" were sometimes advertised in newspapers and drew hundreds (and even thousands) of white spectators, including elected officials and prominent citizens who were so swept up in the carnivals of death that they posed with their children for keepsake photographs within arm's length of mutilated black corpses. "The threat of death by lynching was far more influential in shaping present-day racial reality than contemporary Americans typically understand," concluded the *Times* editorial.

It's essential for Americans to be reminded of this appalling history of persecution because, as we're often reminded, those who don't learn from the past are doomed to repeat it. And when society allows one group to be brutalized, it puts our entire social fabric in danger. In April 1963, as Dr. Martin Luther King sat in a small jail cell in Alabama, he wrote to his supporters, "Injustice anywhere is a threat to justice everywhere. We are caught in an inescapable network of mutuality, tied in a single garment of destiny. Whatever affects one directly, affects all indirectly." King's searing insight burns just as brightly today.

The American civil rights movement benefited enormously from the activism and generosity of Jewish Americans. Victims of prejudice throughout their long history, Americans of Jewish descent knew that the scourge of intolerance in the American South also put them at risk. In fact, one of the more notorious twentieth-century Southern lynchings took place in

Marietta, Georgia, in 1915, when a young Jewish factory manager named Leo Frank was falsely accused of murdering a female employee. During his trial, people gathered outside the courthouse, screaming, "Hang the Jew!" Frank was later dragged from his jail cell by a mob and hung. Even though members of the lynch mob were well-known and included several prominent members of the Marietta community, nobody was ever charged with Frank's murder.

It would take more than seventy years before the Georgia Board of Pardons and Paroles finally granted a posthumous pardon to Leo Frank. Not only was he an innocent man, the pardon declared, but the state of Georgia had "failed to protect him and . . . failed to bring his killers to justice."

Anti-Semitism was not just a stain on the South. Its poison was spread throughout the country by prominent figures like well-known American car manufacturer Henry Ford. A notorious anti-Semite, Ford financed the publication of reams of hateful literature blaming the world's ills on the "International Jew."

Ford and Adolf Hitler formed a mutual admiration society, with the car-maker accepting the highest medal that Nazi Germany could bestow on a foreigner, the Grand Cross of the German Eagle, in July 1938—four months after the German annexation of Austria—and Ford striving to keep the United States from declaring war on Hitler's regime. "I regard Henry Ford as my inspiration," Hitler once told a *Detroit News* reporter as he began his fateful ascent to power, explaining why he kept a life-size portrait of the American automaker next to his desk.

Hitler took the scapegoat strategy to terrifying extremes, creating an exterminationist ideology and putting it into practice with an efficient, German-engineered assembly line of death. From this point on in history, we realized the full horror that human beings were capable of producing if intolerance was given free rein and left unchecked.

This is why I wake up every day now wondering how far the current campaign of Islamophobia and hatred of my fellow Muslims will reach. How much of the toxic speech is just hot air, and how much is prelude to even darker times? Every day, a vocal minority in the media and political elites feels increasingly empowered to smear, caricature, and blatantly lie about Islam and Muslims in order to advance their warped agenda.

From the Crusades to the Holocaust to the Cold War to the current "clash of civilizations," the demonization of "the other" has played a central and nefarious role in justifying the most evil human enterprises. Instead of finding common ground with those of different beliefs, backgrounds, and cultures than ourselves, we crow these days about our American "exceptionalism" and seek to impose our values on those who reject them. This is the pathway to permanent war—a path that has led to enormous wealth and power for the few, and deepening misery for the rest of humanity.

According to Imam Zaid Shakir of Zaytuna College: "The same mindset and political motivations that led to the genocide against the Native Americans, enslavement of African Americans, exclusion of Chinese Americans, internment of Japanese Americans, the prison industrial complex, the 'new Jim Crow,' and calls for denying birthright citizenship to Latinos, are the same forces pushing the so-called Islamophobia agenda."

Almost 1,400 years ago, from the top of Mount Arafat near Mecca, the Prophet Muhammad (peace be upon him) reminded every Muslim in his final sermon:

All mankind is from Adam and Eve, an Arab has no superiority over a non-Arab nor a non-Arab has any superiority over an Arab; also a white has no superiority over black nor a black has any superiority over white except by piety and good action.

There is no superiority in massive military firepower; there is no "exceptionalism" in the degradation of our fellow human beings. It is high time for all people of conscience, regardless of their beliefs, to regain our moral compass before it's too late and we plunge further into the abyss.

Then only God can help us.

* * *

My dear friend Leon Wieseltier is an acclaimed public intellectual, probably most well-known for serving as *The New Republic* literary editor for over three decades. He currently serves as the Isaiah Berlin Senior Fellow for Culture and Policy at the Brookings Institution and as a contributing editor for *The Atlantic* magazine. Here are some cooler facts about Leon's life: He was once honored by being invited to throw out the first pitch at a Washington Nationals baseball game (to commemorate the one hundredth anniversary of The New Republic). And he appeared in an episode of *The Sopranos,* in which his character (Stewart Silverman) got to utter the immortal phrase "a motherfucking year," when someone asked him how long he was on the waiting list for his Mercedes SL-55 convertible—which had just been stolen during a wedding celebration.

I had the honor of sharing the stage with Leon Wieseltier for two years in a row at the 2014 and 2015 Aspen Ideas Festival, to discuss the intersection of religion, culture, and politics in our tempestuous world. "It's good that in America people no longer want to murder

Jews, but to marry them," Leon quipped during the 2014 panel, quoting Irving Kristol.

"We hope to get there one day," I replied, during our discussion of the changing public perceptions of our respective religions, Judaism and Islam.

The following year, Leon and I were paired onstage at the Aspen festival for a discussion titled "Anti-Semitism, Islamophobia and the Future of Religious Racism," during which we discussed the global rise of both anti-Semitism and Islamophobia, the exploitation of religious intolerance by right-wing political forces in Europe and America, and how inter-Abrahamic alliances can help to counter these worrying trends around the world.

"I think the first point that we should make," said Leon during his opening remarks, "[is that] if you want to understand anti-Semitism, don't study the Jews. Study the non-Jews. If you want to understand racism, don't study blacks. Study whites. And if you want to understand Islamophobia, don't study the Muslims. Study the people who are attacking the Muslims."

As long as Jews, Muslims, and blacks were seen as problematic—instead of the prejudice that was directed against them—these minority groups would continue to be stigmatized, said Leon. "If you want to understand hatred, you have to study the people who do the hating—not the people who are the hated."

Leon expressed hope that Muslims in Europe and America would ultimately, like earlier Jewish diasporas, gain a secure foothold in Western societies. Jews in the West, he noted, had successfully "built institutions of self-defense and gained a great degree of security that is unimaginable by the standards of Jewish history." This same process of empowerment and integration will ultimately happen with Western Muslims as well, Leon predicted.

"You know, I assume that in the Muslim communities of Queens, there are Muslim parents who are really upset that their kids no longer speak Urdu or Arabic," Leon remarked. "I remember this [happened within our Jewish communities]. This is the American story. And there is something comforting about the idea that America will do for the Muslims what it did for the Jews and what it did for the Catholics. . . . The problem is that it takes time." In the meantime, he acknowledged, it was exceedingly difficult for Muslim spokespersons like myself to defend our faith and speak out for tolerance, because we are "living in an era that is deeply inflamed about Islam and Muslims" throughout the Western world.

During my remarks that day, I pointed to Barack Obama's election to show how openly Muslims are denigrated in our society today. "In my opinion, whenever people say that Barack Obama is a Muslim, that is their way of saying, 'Barack Obama is black,'" I commented.

"That is their way of 'other-izing' him in way that is currently acceptable in today's American sociopolitical zeitgeist."

Leon and I strived to make our audience see the xenophobic similarities between anti-Semitism and Islamophobia and how our respective religions, with their common Abrahamic traditions, could become allies in the fight against the poisonous spread of intolerance. The current political backlash against Muslims in Europe, we pointed out, follows similar historical patterns of deep-seated anti-Semitism in modern history.

"In Europe, it was perfectly legitimate for a political candidate to run on a platform of anti-Semitism," Leon observed. "You didn't have to pretend that you were concerned about jobs—you could simply say that you were against the Jews." Considering Europe's abysmal historical record when it comes to the treatment of minority groups, he added, there is no surprise for him when he hears about new eruptions of hatred and xenophobia in the cradle of Western civilization. "I am never disappointed in Europe," said Leon, "because I expect nothing of Europe [with] regard [to tolerance and compassion.] Nothing."

I pointed out to Leon that Muslims in Europe are now suffering the same blatant prejudice that Jews once faced. "You talked about how, in Europe's historical past, you had politicians whose sole platform was one of anti-Semitism. Now we are seeing politicians in Europe whose sole platform is Islamophobia."

"Absolutely," Leon said and nodded in agreement.

Leon joked that the absence of any actual evidence of a Muslim takeover of the West "proves how deep the [radical Islam] conspiracy is."

We discussed the various types of official harassment and rebuke aimed at Muslims in Europe, including the 2004 French ban of the hijab and the 2009 prohibition in "neutral" Switzerland against building mosque minarets.

Leon noted that the 2004 French headscarf ban was a perfect example of the difference between Europe—particularly France, where "universalism is coercive"—and the looser attitudes in America. Of course, with hijab-wearing women now being attacked on the streets of the United States, perhaps the American way of treating religious differences is no more enlightened. Leon also cogently noted the hypocrisy of French society, which has no problem bringing religion into the public sphere, when it comes to government subsidies for Catholic schools.

France's institutionalized religious bias is "wrong," continued Leon. "They are so threatened about their own religious identity and their own French identity, that they fear that the expression of a Muslim identity in the public square will somehow endanger it further—which I always find outrageous."

When I asked Leon what European governments can do to combat anti-Semitism and Islamophobia, he replied, "I actually don't like laws against hate speech. . . . I think it should not be against the law in Germany to say that the Holocaust was a hoax," adding that this opinion probably put him in the minority of modern Jewish public intellectuals today.

"I believe in free speech," Leon continued. "I really do believe in free speech. And I think that open societies were designed for the giving and taking of offense." He finally noted that everyone in Western societies needed to thicken their skin when it comes to free speech within our global marketplace of ideas.

Leon and I then shifted our focus from Europe to our own country. I observed that living in a liberal democracy with a strong Constitutional tradition of religious freedom gave American Muslims a unique ability to practice Islam more freely than in any country in the world—including the fifty-seven Muslim-majority nations on the face of the Earth. Having said that, our conversation quickly turned to rising Islamophobia in America and the ridiculous campaign to block Islamic law from somehow taking over the US of A.

"I am always amused—although amused is too kind a word—when I hear about Jews worrying about Sharia coming to America," remarked Leon Wieseltier. "Because orthodox Jews resort to rabbinical courts all the time. There is a vast network of rabbinical courts in this country. They are sophisticated judicial institutions. They base themselves entirely on Halacha—the body of Jewish law. They pose no threat to American Jewish citizenship in this country. And so the hypocrisy of those people always puts me out."

Considering the shared roots of our two Abrahamic religions, and the deep injustices that people of our faiths faced today, I interjected that I found it particularly distressing when I hear "anti-Semitism within the Muslim community and see Islamophobia within the Jewish community."

"Doubly painful," lamented Leon.

"To me, it marks the victory of majority societies," I continued.

"—to turn us [Jews and Muslims] against each other," Leon said, completing my sentence. "You know, in the Jewish tradition, the basis for social compassion and social solidarity is the memory of one's own experience of persecution. Solidarity always requires imagination. You have to be able to imagine the predicament of people whose lives are other than your own." He further noted that public intellectuals sometimes have to remind their respective communities that even though everyone has been the "oppressed" group in the past, so too have all of our respective communities been the "oppressors" as well.

Leon further warned us against placing collective guilt upon entire religious faiths for the violent acts of minority fringe elements. He then proceeded to tell our audience at the 2015 Aspen Ideas Festival about the story of Baruch Goldstein, an American Jewish doctor who murdered twenty-nine Palestinians (and injured one-hundred-and-twenty-five more) while they said their morning *fajr* prayers at the Cave of the Patriarchs mosque in the West Bank city of Hebron in February 1994. It was a horrific act of religious terrorism that hit painfully close to home for my dear friend Leon.

"A Jew who went to the [same] yeshiva that I went to when I was a boy savagely murdered Palestinians in Hebron in 1994," Leon told our captivated audience. But Judaism was not the culprit that day. "It is not the case that an act of violence is representative of an entire religion," he said. Nonetheless, added Leon, although not all Jewish people should be held responsible for the vile acts of Baruch Goldstein, there is still a need for our religious communities to self-reflect when acts of terrorism do occur in our respective names.

"I was very clear that those of us who come from that [religious] background have to take responsibility and see if something was wrong," said Leon. "But the idea that Baruch Goldstein's act 'exemplified' Judaism is preposterous. . . . Preposterous!"

"I think we have to be more sophisticated in our understanding of what these religions are," he concluded. "They are complicated entities. They are civilizations. And every civilization includes everything—including violence. There is no great monotheistic religion that has not been responsible for the perpetration of violence or the killing of innocent individuals [in its name]. There is no such religion."

Since Judaism and Islam represent two-thirds of the Abrahamic religious trifecta, it would behoove our predominantly Christian Western societies to address Islamophobia in the same way that our Western nations have addressed anti-Semitism in our historical past. People from all backgrounds must acknowledge that our human race has far more similarities than we have differences and that all forms of modern-day racism, xenophobia, and bigotry need to be addressed lest we repeat the tragic lessons from the ghosts of scapegoats past.

Because history always teaches us that there will always be another demonized minority group who will become "the other" tomorrow. Our human race seems tragically doomed to keep finding scapegoat minorities on whom the majority can vent its fears and frustrations. This demonization creates an inevitable cycle of bloodshed and revenge. But as the means of violence and weapons of destruction become increasingly terrifying, we must find our common humanity before we annihi-late ourselves into collective oblivion.

Because there is no "Us versus Them" in our increas-ingly shrinking global village. There is only "Us." As my friend Leon told me that day in Aspen: "This is not a clash of civilizations . . . because every civilization con-tains the clash within itself."

But in these dark times, we must also hold within ourselves the impossible dream of elusive peace for all people. May the God whom we all share grant us the wisdom to achieve it together.